Teaching a
Young Actor

OTHER BOOKS BY RENÉE HARMON

How to Audition for Movies and TV
The Beginning Filmmaker's Guide to Directing
The Beginning Filmmaker's Business Guide

Teaching a Young Actor

How to Train Children of All Ages for Success in Movies, TV, and Commercials

Renée Harmon

Walker and Company
New York

Copyright © 1994 by Renée Harmon

First published in the United States of America in 1994 by Walker
Publishing Company, Inc.

Published simultaneously in Canada by Thomas Allen & Son Canada,
Limited, Markham, Ontario

Library of Congress Cataloging-in-Publication Data
Harmon, Renée.
Teaching a young actor : how to train children of all ages for
success in movies, TV, and commercials / Renée Harmon.
p. cm.
Published simultaneously in Canada by Thomas Allen & Son Canada,
Markham, Ontario.
Includes bibliographical references and index.
ISBN 0-8027-7423-7 (pbk.)
1. Children as actors.   2. Acting—Study and teaching.   I. Title.
PN3157.H37   1994
792'.028'083—dc20   94-1425
CIP

Book design by Claire Naylon Vaccaro

Printed in the United States of America

2   4   6   8   10   9   7   5   3   1

Contents

PART ONE.   Introducing the Fun of Acting: Basic Acting Techniques

PART TWO.   On-camera Techniques

Contents vii

PART SIX.   *A*uditioning

Preface

Teaching a Young Actor has been written for the acting teacher who prepares child actors for film, TV, and commercials, and for the parent who lacks the opportunity of taking his or her child to acting classes. This book also has been written for the teacher and/or recreational counselor who wishes to enrich a program of activities for children. It has been written for the parent who may not necessarily want to see his or her child on-screen but looks for ways to make the youngster more outgoing and assertive. And this book has been written for the therapist whose job it is to "unlock" a child's emotions.

Teaching a Young Actor is based upon my experience as an actress, a director, a motion picture producer, and an instructor. (Since 1978 I have had the privilege of teaching an experimental children's acting class, Acting and Expression, for the California State University Northridge Extension.) Students—whether they are actors, are working toward becoming actors, or are simply attending acting classes to become more self-confident—have to learn about themselves. Only then can they express emotions effectively within the boundaries of the written script. Only then will they become more confident in the way they express themselves and relate to others.

The acting techniques explained in Part 1, such as Positive and Negative Reactions, Intensity Levels, Points of Attention, and Thoughts, may be new to some of you and therefore have been dealt with in detail.

These exercises give the young actor the technical tools for the straightforward acting techniques that motion pictures, TV, and commercials now demand.

But equally important, these exercises teach shy, introverted children to become more outgoing and assertive, and help them to overcome the emotional hurdles of poor self-concept and poor communication skills.

Should you be teaching children who plan to become professional actors, it will prove helpful to use the sessions in sequence, as presented. Yet depending on your teaching goal (professional, recreational, therapeutic), *all sessions can be taught independently from the others*. The program is a flexible one, and each session need not follow the plan in a strict order of events. To make things a little easier, an introduction explaining the purpose and goals of the sessions precedes each part of the book.

Acknowledgments

I wish to express my gratitude to Mary Kennan Herbert for her never-failing enthusiasm in this book, as well as for her helpful suggestions. I wish to thank James J. O'Donnell, dean of the California State University Northridge Extension, for his interest in my Acting and Expression classes for children; Peg Auchterlonie for her strong support; and Dr. Jane Fulz for this stimulating course, which is so different from conventional acting instruction.

Also I wish to thank my daughter, Cheryl Harmon, for introducing some of the Exercises for the Very Young Child to the children of the Shadow Ranch Park Pre-School (Los Angeles Park and Recreation Division), and Paulette Paulson for patiently typing the manuscript from a draft that sometimes must have looked like hieroglyphics.

PART ONE

Introducing the Fun of Acting: Basic Acting Techniques

Getting to Know One Another

During the first session of an acting class for children, you do not want to overwhelm students with any "acting" exercises. After all, the purpose of the acting technique you are teaching, the one we will discuss in this book, has been designed to lead the children away from "actorly" expressions and toward the roots of honest and natural screen behavior.

After everyone has settled down, place your students in a semicircle around you and announce that everyone will be given the opportunity to tell a short story. You may suggest topics such as

Hobbies
Pets
Sports
Vacations
Friends
Favorite subject in school

Allow each child two to three minutes to tell a story. Some children may need a little gentle coaching. I have found the following remarks helpful: "That sounds interesting. . . . What happened next? . . . And then?"

Once the child has finished the story, smile and nod to let the child know you appreciated his or her efforts. Refrain (at times difficult to do) from either complimenting or critiquing any child, but make your group aware that you give each of them your full attention.

Your next step is to encourage the children to speak about their feelings regarding the related story. Expect that most children are reluctant to do so and at times are even afraid to speak. Some refuse to deal with their emotions. This reluctance is the root both of "hammy" and therefore dishonest acting and of the fear of standing up for oneself and making one's opinion known. Don't be disappointed if in answer to your question "How did you feel when your parents told you they were going to take you to Mexico for a vacation?" you elicit nothing more than a shrug and a noncommittal "I don't know." Or perhaps your query "Weren't you happy to get a puppy for your birthday?" will be answered with a solemn "I guess so."

You may be tempted to prod your students to more expressive responses, but refrain from doing so. Prodding and coaching will only make your students tense during this introductory session. Let things go. Show yourself as the kind and happy person you are, and sooner or later (probably sooner) your students will open up to you.

Do not expect the children to confess to any feelings, whether of happiness, fear, anger, or sadness, but turn on your faithful VCR and watch with your students a segment (about ten to fifteen minutes) of an "I Love Lucy" show. You, of course, have chosen a segment that shows emotions and gives you the opportunity to ask: "What did Lucy *do* when Ricky said or did this or that?" (It is important that you make your group aware of the segment's *action*; that is, find out whether your students know what happened in the scene.)

After you have established the action, ask, "What do you think Lucy *felt* when she did or said this or that?"

Permit the children to discuss (and argue) among themselves as they discover whether Lucy was *happy* or *angry* or *confused* before you ask, "How could you tell?" End the session with this advice: "Actors, regardless of whether they're onstage or on-screen, have to make the audience *aware of their emotions.*"

Tips *to Help the Very Young Child*

Asking the very young child to tell a little story is a major undertaking but enjoyable. Finding a topic is the first difficulty. Most likely, as with the older group, you will have to suggest a topic. I found out that pets and toys are favored, while vacation or preschool experiences are too complex for the very young child to relate to. If children are reluctant to talk or seem to be at a loss, you may gently prod them with the same kinds of questions you used on your older group. After all, it is important that you make very young children feel secure and proud of whatever they relate to you.

Don't ever ask your very young group to speak about any *emotion* experienced regarding their puppy or favorite toy. Children in this age group experience very strong emotions but are unable to relate their feelings verbally.

Toward the end of the session (sessions for the very young child should not exceed one hour) let them enjoy a funny (not violent) cartoon or a segment of "The Muppet Show" and ask, "What did _____ do?"

Most likely you'll have to help your students a little with their answers, and if you are rewarded with "Miss Piggy climbed to the roof" or "The cat chased the dog" or "The birdie flew away and laughed," you ought to be highly satisfied, but if you do not get much of a response, don't worry. The aim of this first session is to make the children comfortable with the new and strange environment of the classroom, studio, or stage, and have them develop a little confidence in you, the teacher. If the little ones have fun and are eager to return to their next session, so much the better.

S E S S I O N 2

What Is Make-believe?

Start this session by having the children run around in a circle, followed by your favorite bend-and-stretch exercises. Once the children have let off some steam and have gathered around you in a semicircle, remind them of the "Lucy" segment they viewed during the previous session, concluding with the question "Who is this Lucy you saw on TV?"

The most common answer will be "I don't know." Some will venture to state that Lucy is Lucille Ball, a famous actress, while others, taking the show more literally, will assert, "Lucy is Ricky's funny wife."

Again, listen to *all* answers attentively. Accept *all* answers as valid before pointing out, "What you see on the screen or on the stage is *make-believe*. The *actress* Lucille Ball portrays—or *plays* (use the terminology closest to your group's comprehension)—the *character* Lucy. The Lucy we see on the screen is a combination of" (hold up a script) "the script, written by the writers, and" (hold up Lucille Ball's photo) "the actress who portrays Lucy on the screen."

At this point it is helpful to have a blackboard handy. Draw this diagram:

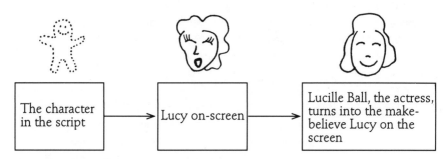

| The character in the script | → | Lucy on-screen | → | Lucille Ball, the actress, turns into the make-believe Lucy on the screen |

Point out that the Lucy on the screen is a character, not a real person. The actress Lucy (the real person) uses her imagination and her emotions to portray this character.

It is a good idea to show the "Lucy" sequence again to discuss Lucy's *actions* (what she does to show her feelings). Now is the time to explain: "To 'make believe' means to make something real that is not real." As you may have guessed, you'll find yourself surrounded by blank faces. Don't be disconcerted but announce, "All right, children, now we will make something real that is not real." Ask your group to think of something they use every day—such as a toothbrush, a pencil, or maybe a mug. (Any item that means something to a child, like a favorite toy, should be avoided.) Ask the children to sit comfortably and to close their eyes. Talk them slowly through their "make-believe" exercise: "Close your eyes. Imagine that the object you have selected is hanging in front of your eyes. Look at your object. Make out its shape and color or colors. Take your time." Pause awhile before continuing. "And now lift your hands and touch the object. Move your fingers around its edges. How does it feel? Does it feel soft? Hard? Does it have edges?"

Give your group plenty of time to work on their individual objects before you ask them to open their eyes. Ask for a show of hands from those for whom the object became "real." A few will admit that they could not make the object real; others will say that sometimes they could feel the object and sometimes they couldn't. Still others (the very sensitive and creative ones) will say that the object *did* seem real. (Of course, a few children will fib.)

At this time suggest that each participant work on visualizing an imaginary object at least once a day.

This exercise has a twofold purpose: It will teach children concentration (an important aspect of the acting craft), and it will prepare them for the more involved exercises covered in Part 3 of this book.

During this session, repeat the above make-believe exercise about three times, choosing a different object each time.

Now the children should be ready to explore more difficult areas.

Wash your hands. Feel the soap, the water, the towel.
Drink something very hot.
Feel wind on your face.
Feel sunshine on your face.
Feel snow on your face.

Tips *to Help the Very Young Child*

Start this session with bend-and-stretch exercises. Announce to your group that they will have fun with "make-believe." Make certain they know what make-believe means. Since the "create an imaginary object" exercise you worked on with the older group is too difficult for the very young child to comprehend, you'll start out this group with the "washing hands" exercise. Unlike the session with older children, for very young children you'll have to talk your group through each step.

Turn on the faucet. Is it difficult to turn? Feel the water flow over your hands. How does the water feel? Does it feel warm? Cold? Hot? Pick up the soap. How does the soap feel in your hand? Is it a real big cake of soap, or just a sliver? Now smell the soap. How does it smell? Rub the soap over your hands and arms. Make lots and lots of lather. How does the soap feel? Slick? Rinse off your hands.

Next have the children tell you about their pets or any animal they have come in contact with. Ask the children to close their eyes as you verbally lead them through the exercise.

There is a kitten or puppy on your lap. Start petting it; feel how soft the fur is. Careful, careful, don't hurt the little thing.

At this time some of your students will be ready to pick objects of their own. Happily accept whatever suggestions the children have to offer, but do not push any of them to contribute.

Reserve the end of this session for the "lollipop break." Hand out lollipops and let your children enjoy them. Ask them to close their eyes and to concentrate on the taste. Then ask them:

How did the candy taste? Sweet? Like strawberry? Like lemon? Like raspberry?

Insist on very specific answers; this is a concentration exercise for the very young child.

SESSION 3

Learn About Yourself (I)

By now you'll have noticed the composition of your group. Most of your children will be attentive and fairly creative and outgoing. They have fun. But invariably you will have some children that demand your special attention. For purposes of illustration, I'll call them Timmy, Mary Ann, and Laura.

Timmy is a bright-eyed, outgoing child. He loves to "perform." He is used to winning the lead part in every school play he auditions for, and he has a charming way of drawing attention to himself. But he confuses the emotion he displays with the emotions he really feels. As a result, as he matures he may—as an actor—be incapable of projecting honest emotions in a simple and believable way. As a person, he may be confused about his feelings toward others.

Mary Ann seems to be the answer to your prayers. Anxiously she discovers whatever is expected of her and diligently does whatever is required. Her actions and reactions are a "performance." Her constant submissive behavior diminishes her self-reliance. Most of her actions and reactions are based on what others expect of her. Her parents, her teachers, and even her peers are the puppeteers. They pull the string, and Mary Ann, the puppet—her self-confidence diminishing with every performance—dances.

Laura is so shy that she hardly dares to whisper her name. For one reason or the other, most likely self-protection, she pulls her shyness like a shell around herself. It doesn't take a crystal ball to tell that if she doesn't change her ways, life will treat her harshly. Unfortunately, she is the typical victim.

These three personality types will require special attention throughout your sessions with them. By now you'll have a pretty clear picture of them. The Timmys have pushed themselves into the foreground. The Mary Anns followed all your instructions but did not display any creativity of their own, and the Lauras tried hard to remain unnoticed. The time has come to give these children more individual attention. Since this and the next session may prove to be emotionally stressful for some of your students, I suggest that you give your group a prolonged warm-up.

After the children have formed a circle, ask them to place both hands on the preceding student's shoulders and play the choo-choo train game, walking in a circle, stomping their feet, and calling "Choo-choo-choo-choo" faster and faster until—"Haaaaaaaaaaaaaaaa"—the train stands still.

Having reached the train station, all children flop onto the floor. After a rest period, begin the "relaxation exercise."

Close your eyes.
Lie there, relaxed.
Take a deep breath.
Let your arms and legs get heavier and heavier. *Feel* how heavy they are.
Imagine that water—all the tension and worries you experienced today—flows from your toes and fingertips. After the water has run out, begin to listen to the sounds around you. Listen, but do not hold on to any of them. Permit your thoughts to run through your mind, but do not hold on to any of them. Enjoy your worry-free, relaxed state of mind.
Open your eyes, sit up, and look forward to today's class.

Next, you hand out a short practice scene. Give everyone enough time to read and absorb the scene.

JULIE/JOHN: I'm really sad today.

CARRIE/CRAIG: So what happened?

JULIE/JOHN: Nothing went right. I got a D in my history exam. I studied like a maniac, but I cannot for the life of me keep those history dates straight. My friend Ida is right; I'm a dunce.

CARRIE/CRAIG: Ida has a big mouth, don't listen to her.

JULIE/JOHN: My aunt Grace tells me again and again I could do better if I were to apply myself. She and Uncle Ralph say I will never amount to anything.

CARRIE/CRAIG: Forget about those two. They stick their big noses into everything.

JULIE/JOHN: And my backhand in tennis is getting worse every day . . . and I try hard to be perfect in tennis and . . . well, everything.

CARRIE/CRAIG: Nothing can be perfect, I've told you so a thousand times.

JULIE/JOHN: I wish I could be like Mary/Mike, outgoing and well liked, good in school, and a terrific tennis player.

Permit the children to perform the scene. (Be careful not to cast your shy Lauras in the part of Julie/John before you ask, "How about telling me a little about this Julie/John? What kind of person do you think she/he is?" Your children will be happy to supply you with all kinds of derogatory descriptions. "She's a whiner"; "She's dumb"; "I don't know how Carrie/Craig can stand his/her friend."

Now it is time to move on to self-concept. Self-concept is the way we see ourselves.

Pass a mirror around and let each child make some simple statements about his or her appearance. "I have brown hair and brown eyes. I wear a red shirt."

End this exercise by congratulating your group. "Terrific! Each and every one of you saw yourselves as you really are. And now let's take a good look what happens if others do not see you as you are." Ask one of the Timmys to volunteer. Hand him the mirror and ask again for a simple appearance statement: "I have brown hair and brown eyes. I wear a red shirt."

Sternly looking at your student, shake your head. "You are all mistaken. Can't you tell what you see in the mirror? You have blond hair and blue eyes and you wear a green shirt."

Timmy, outgoing as he is, will have a great time contradicting you, until you finally give in: "Naturally, you have brown hair and brown eyes, and do wear a red shirt. What Timmy showed you is that you have to see yourself as you really are, and not as others see you. This goes for your personality and achievements as well." Ask each child to talk about a subject in school, a task performed at home, or a favorite hobby or sport. Each student should preface his or her remark with "I'm proud of myself because I . . ."

I always try to repeat the mirror exercise with my Mary Anns and Lauras before I go to the following segment.

Pair off your students and have them look at one another and make flattering remarks about one another's looks and outfits. "You have brown hair, and it is really shiny. Your eyes have such a happy sparkle. I can tell you like to laugh. And your red shirt is really neat."

After all this preliminary work, you are ready to explain self-concept. Give reasons why it is important to have a good self-concept. "The word 'self-concept' refers to the picture we have about ourselves. You have looked into the mirror and described exactly what you saw. That was fine. But self-concept deals not only with looks but also with what we think about our achievements. Naturally, we compare ourselves with others, and in some areas we can do better than they do and in other areas they do better than we do. That is all right—in fact, it's exactly how things ought to be. Now let's look at Julie/John's self-concept. Is it high, medium, or low?"

Everyone will agree that Julie/John's self-concept is low, and you will point out the areas that have caused the low self-concept:

Julie/John strives for perfection.
She/he believes all the detrimental (bad) things others say about her/him.
Julie/John believes she/he cannot do anything right.

If necessary, you may go on with these questions:

Why does Julie/John feel this way about herself/himself?
Is this right or wrong?

Why do you think she/he listens to people who put her/him down?
Has anyone (Aunt Grace and Uncle Ralph) the right to do so?

End with this statement: "No one and nothing in life can be perfect. Try to do as well as you can, but do not strive for perfection." Then pose the question "Why do you think she/he wants perfection?"

The answer, no doubt, will be, "Julie/John wants to be liked by others." Applaud your group, and add, "But no one will like Julie/John until they like themselves. It is very simple: Self-concept may be compared with a cat chasing its tail. The way you see yourself is the way you present yourself (show yourself) to others. They, in turn, will see you the way you see yourself and will treat you accordingly."

It is a great help to have a blackboard handy as you continue your lecture.

"Imagine you are invited to a party; you want to make new friends, and you know you'll meet many new people there. Remember, people will see you not as you really are but as they *perceive* you—the way *you present yourself.* The way you present yourself depends on the way you see yourself."

Draw a diagram on the blackboard. "This is what happens if you have a good self-concept:

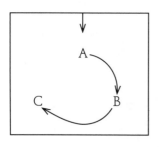

A. You look forward to making new friends. You know you are a likable person, and people will like you. You approach others and talk to them.

B. Others will like you and appreciate your efforts to get to know them. They will gladly accept you into their group.

C. You feel good about yourself. Your self-concept increases."

"But now take a good look at what happens if you have a poor self-concept:

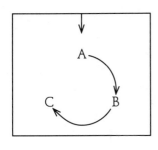

A. You want to make new friends, but you are afraid that no one will like you. 'The others are so much smarter than I am. Why should they bother with me?'

B. You do not approach others but hope that someone will come up to you. Others may feel you are stuck-up, and they will ignore you.

C. You think that since no one pays attention to you, you are unworthy. Your self-concept drops even lower."

Before we go on to the next session, let me add a little advice. Even though these sessions on self-concept are extremely important for the Lauras and Mary Anns in your group, never ever point out children for their shyness. On the contrary, make every effort to encourage and compliment these children. They need it.

Have the children repeat in unison:

People will not see me as I am. People will see me the way I present myself. The way I present myself depends on the way I see myself. I am who I am, and *I am proud* of myself.

Ask the children to jot down these lines, or give them printed cards to tape on their mirror and look at every day.

Arrange your students in groups of five. "Now let's play the party game. You just moved to a new neighborhood, and you are invited to a birthday party. You do not know any of the kids present. Go up to them and start talking."

Introduce yourself.
  Tell them that you just moved to this neighborhood.
  Tell them where you came from (but don't brag, and don't compare your new town with your previous one).
  Tell them how pleased you are to have been invited.
  Find something you can admire about the party, the new school, or the new town.

Let each of the five actors (paying attention that the Timmys don't start bragging) play the role of the newcomer.

End this session with the joyful recitation of "I am who I am, and I'm proud of myself."

S E S S I O N   4

Learn About Yourself (II)

Begin this session with the now familiar recitation of "I am who I am and I'm proud of myself."

"And now we will take a little time to talk about ourselves and to appreciate ourselves."

"You mean brag?" one might volunteer.

"It is not nice to brag" will be another response.

You answer, "That's true. It is not nice to boast about things we may have that others lack. But appreciating our strengths and accomplishments is *not* bragging."

(It is important that you teach your students the basics of a healthy self-concept, one that helps them be proud of themselves and their accomplishments. Unfortunately, actors—whether children or adults—have to face rejections and only those whose personalities are based on a sound self-concept will be able to deal with disappointments.)

And now repeat the pride exercise the children are already familiar with from the previous session. Ask everyone to share "two great things about me" with the class. These accomplishments, remind them, need not be awe-inspiring, just things they are proud of.

Continue the discussion by asking the following questions:

Tell me in what way you have grown in the past year. (Maybe you keep your temper more under control, maybe you help around the house more, maybe you do your homework more diligently.)

What have you accomplished during the past year? (Every little thing counts; do not ask your students to concentrate on big accomplishments.)

Make a list of friends and relatives who think you are great.

Think about one or two things you may improve upon (being more attentive in school, keeping your room neat).

For the second part of this session, announce a fun improvisation—Little Red Riding Hood and the Big Bad Wolf.

Immediately you will hear groans and complaints of "That's baby stuff," which you squelch by explaining that this exercise illustrates self-concept. "You all remember the story of Little Red Riding Hood. Walking through the forest, carrying a basket of goodies to her sick grandmother, she meets the wolf. During our first improvisation she is very much afraid; she knows she cannot defend herself against the wolf. Her self-concept is . . ."

"Poor" is the immediate answer.

"All right. Act out this poor self-concept." You demonstrate hunched shoulders and a shy little smile.

"And how is the wolf's self-concept?"

"Terrific. He knows he can scare Little Red." Let the children act out the self-concept by growling and flexing their biceps.

Now they are in the mood to have fun *and* to do a good acting job on the previously disdained "baby stuff." Team up your group into twos. It doesn't matter whether a boy plays Little Red Riding Hood and girls play the wolf. All of the actors will be given the chance to play both parts. Do not forget to repeat the acting out before the roles are reversed, so that the wolf's self-concept is now low and Little Red Riding Hood's is high. Remind your group that the dialogue is not nearly as important as feeling and showing their self-concept.

One of the most delightful examples of Little Red Riding Hood's good self-concept was created by two eight-year-olds. It went something like this:

WOLF: What are you doing in the dark and dangerous forest?

LITTLE RED RIDING HOOD: I'm taking a cake to my sick grandmother.

Sighing deeply, the wolf looks at the cake.

WOLF: This cake looks yummy-yum.

He licks his lips, then puts his hand on his stomach.

WOLF: I'm so hungry my stomach hurts.

LITTLE RED RIDING HOOD: Sorry to hear that. But, well, I must be going. Nice to have met you, Mr. Wolf.

WOLF: Please give me your cake; I'm so hungry.

LITTLE RED RIDING HOOD: Sorry, that cake is for my grandmother.

WOLF: How about a slice of cake; a tiny one?

LITTLE RED RIDING HOOD: No chance.

WOLF: But I'm hungry. I have not eaten for two days.

LITTLE RED RIDING HOOD: Go to the store and buy something.

WOLF: I have no money.

LITTLE RED RIDING HOOD: Earn some. Get a job.

WOLF: I cannnot find a job. People hire cats and dogs, but no wolves. People don't like wolves.

LITTLE RED RIDING HOOD: Then change your personality. Get a better self-concept.

WOLF: How?

LITTLE RED RIDING HOOD: Come to this acting class.

WOLF: They won't take me in.

Tips *to Help the Very Young Child*

The "get to know yourself exercises," needless to say, are too difficult and boring for younger children. But the Little Red Riding Hood and the Big Bad Wolf exercise, besides being lots of fun, will teach the very young child to be outgoing and stand up for himself or herself.

SESSION 5

The Actor's Positive and Negative Reactions (I)

Hand out the next practice scene. Calling attention to the phrases in italics, which indicate how Julie/John has changed, ask your group to perform the scene.

JULIE/JOHN: I had a miserable day today. (*Acknowledges and accepts his/her mood.*)

CARRIE/CRAIG: So what happened?

JULIE/JOHN: I got a D in my history exam. I studied like a maniac—no, to be honest, I should've studied more instead of going to the movies. (*Faces reality.*) I know I have trouble remembering dates. (*States facts, but does not feel sorry for himself/herself.*)

CARRIE/CRAIG: Says who?

JULIE/JOHN: Did I ever tell you that my aunt Grace told everyone I would never amount to anything? Well, I will show her. . . . (*Does not permit Aunt Grace to browbeat him/her; determined to "show her"; does not permit another's opinion to influence his/her self-concept.*)

CARRIE/CRAIG: Who listens to her anyway?

JULIE/JOHN: And I have to improve in tennis. I know I won't ever be as terrific as Mary/Mike, but there is room for improvement. (*Realizes own limitations, and does not try to be perfect.*)

After discussing Julie/John's new self-concept and making certain that your students grasp the idea of good self-concept, ask them to perform both practice scenes. Then ask how they felt playing Julie/John.

You will get answers like "I felt sad," "I felt angry," "I felt so helpless while acting the first scene," but "I felt confident," "I felt happy," or "I felt good" performing the second scene.

Remind your group that nothing but Julie/John's self-concept changed during the second scene, and point out the importance of the fact that *the way things are is not as important as the way we look at things.*

Now the actual acting training begins. Point out to your group that even though they stated they were sad or angry during scene I and happy and confident during scene II, you the audience could not detect much difference in the way they performed the scene. From there go on to explain that every actor, whether child or adult, must be able to project a variety of moods and emotions in a clear but natural way. No actor should portray any emotion he or she does not feel. If this happens, the actor portrays an "attitude" and not an honestly felt emotion. On the other hand, it is a fallacy to believe that every honestly felt emotion will register on the screen or on the stage.

From today's session on, your students should learn not only to *feel* emotions but to *project* them as well. So far you have made them aware that it is okay to be proud of oneself and one's accomplishments. You have given them tools that teach them to stand up for themselves and their opinions. Hopefully the Lauras in your class have become more outgoing, and the Mary Anns have lost some of their rigidity. Your Timmys, undoubtedly, are hamming it up even more. Don't worry about them. All the following sessions will lead them in the right direction.

"And now," you inform your group, "we will do a commercial. This commercial is about milk. Show me how good milk tastes." This is the text:

Milk.
I like milk.
Milk is great.

Tape this "commercial." As you and your group view the tape, you will discover that only a few of the children display any vitality. Some children will be "deadpan," others will be "acty," and others will try very hard to smile even though they are uncomfortable in front of the camera. Point out that only a few, if any, of the commercials would entice anyone to buy a gallon of milk.

"Why?"

"Because no one felt happy about drinking milk."

"Come on," cries one of your students, "this is acting. We have to pretend, not feel."

"Wrong, you have to feel, not pretend." You go on. "If you are happy about something, your body is relaxed and you smile."

Another student tries to "catch" you: "But if I don't like milk, I pretend, and you just said one should feel, and *not* pretend."

"You should, whether or not you like milk, put your body into the same condition as if you were to like milk."

Don't worry about all the faces staring blankly at you. Continue with: "What we are speaking about is an acting technique called *positive and negative reactions*. Your brain knows whether a situation is reality or make-believe but, strangely enough, your body doesn't. For instance, if you use the technique of *positive reaction*, you will have a believably happy performance even though you have butterflies in your stomach as you step onstage or in front of a camera."

Make your student aware that showing emotion is not only important to the actor but also imperative for our day-to-day relationships. You might use the following example: "Imagine that you have saved a long time to buy your friend a birthday gift. You can hardly wait for him/her to open the package because you know you have bought the perfect gift, something your friend will cherish. But what disappointment—your friend does not seem to be impressed. What most likely happened is that he/she loves your gift but is unable to express delight." Or—"a friend asks you to help him/her cheat on an exam. You are determined not to, but if your answer is weak or wishy-washy, how does your friend know you are serious?"

In life as well as on-screen we have to let people know how we feel. "In life— and in acting—we have only two basic emotions. We either like something or we dislike something; that means we are either *positive* or *negative*. A positive emotion is caused by your happiness about something, while a negative emotion is caused by fear, anger, or sadness. Now remember, to every motive—something that causes your happiness, anger, fear, or sadness—your body will react appropriately. If you are positive (happy), your body will be relaxed and you smile; if you are sad, angry, or afraid, your body will grow tense. First let's practice positives.

"Lie down on the floor. Take a long, deep breath and let it out slowly. Stretch. Lie as comfortably as possible. Close your eyes. Do you remember our 'make-believe' exercises from the other day? Good. Imagine it is the first day of your vacation. No school to go to, no homework to worry over, no chores to do, just freedom—wonderful freedom. You are lying in a meadow. Feel sunshine on your face. Listen to the sounds surrounding you—crickets, birds, and the murmur of a small stream. Smell the fragrant grass. Now open your eyes, get up, and stretch. How do you feel?"

There is no question about it: Everyone feels relaxed and happy. Most likely you see smiles on your students' faces. Ask your group to be observant of their bodies as they go through the next exercise.

"Now make believe that you are in class and that you're going to take a test. See the paper in front of you. This might be a history, math, or French test. Pick a subject that is causing you problems.

"Have you picked a subject? Do you see the test in front of you? All right, let me talk you through it. Try to feel the emotions I suggest to you.

"You do not dare to look at the test. You know the test will be difficult and you won't get a passing grade. But you have to take the test. You force yourself to take a deep breath. You have studied; you'll do your best. Now take a good look at the paper in front of you—and what do you know—it is easy. You know you can do it. Take another big, happy breath, pick up your imaginary pencil, and start working."

Repeat to your students: "When you are positive you relax, smile, then speak." Warn them not to speak and smile simultaneously but relax, smile, and speak.

> Relax, smile, and speak: Count to ten.
>
> Relax, smile, and speak: "Jack and Jill went up a hill to fetch a pail of water. Jack fell down, and broke his crown, and Jill came tumbling after."

Now the children are ready to repeat their milk commercial. You will be surprised how much more alive and natural the performances are. After viewing the tape, congratulate your students on their performances, give some gentle advice where applicable, and close your session by saying, "Now we all have learned how to do a commercial. At home, when you watch TV, pay close attention to whether the actors do their jobs right."

Tips *to Help the Very Young Child*

Announce in today's session that "we all will practice *big, happy smiles,* and later we will do a commercial, like a commercial you see on TV."

> Do stretch-and-bend exercises.
>
> Do the choo-choo train exercise. Have children hold on to each other's shoulders and stomp around in a circle—choo-choo-choo—making certain that the children inhale and exhale thoroughly.
>
> Ask the children to take another deep breath, drop their shoulders, and let their arms dangle. Then you explain: "The way you feel now is called *relaxed*. Please repeat after me: Relaxed. Relaxed. Relaxed."
>
> Ask the children to smile happily. Some children will smile delightedly, others will grin in a tense way, and others may even frown. Do not comment on the smiles. Do not discourage anyone.

Immediately practice the milk commercial with your group.

Milk.
I like milk.
Milk is great.

"And now you'll do the commercial in front of the camera. You all have seen a video camera before? Okay. Now imagine this camera is your best friend, and you tell him or her how good milk tastes. You want your friend to drink milk."

Make certain you talk the little ones through the taping, as follows:

Relax.
Smile—give me a great big smile.
Now say after me:
> Milk.
> I like milk.
> Milk is great.

Next, place three items on the table: a doll, a book, and a game. Ask your very young group to pick up the doll and smile a little, and say, "I like the doll." Then have them pick up the book, smile a bigger smile, and say, "I like the book." And finally, have them pick up the game, smile a great big smile, and say, "I like the game."

SESSION 6

The Actor's Positive and Negative Reactions (II)

Begin this session by reminding your students of the sequence of *relax, smile,* and *speak* in a positive reaction; let them repeat (not on camera) the milk commercial.

Then say, "As I mentioned during the last session, your brain knows the difference between reality and make-believe; your body does not. For this reason your body reacts to a fictional situation—the situation the character you portray finds himself or herself in—exactly the same way as if it were a real situation. Much unbelievable acting is the result of actors' inability to involve their bodies. So many actors act with their faces only. But in life one's body is always involved; it grows tense when we are negative and relaxed when we are positive. For this reason an emotion cannot be portrayed in any believable way if the actor's body language conflicts with what the character feels.

"Imagine yourself having been cast for a movie in which you have to portray a character who has just received the most wonderful news. If this is your first acting assignment, it is understandable if you are nervous. Naturally your, the actor's, body will be tense, while the character's body is supposed to be relaxed. Without any doubt, the following will happen: You are fully aware of not fulfilling your acting assignment. As a result, you will start *pushing* the character's emotion, that is to say, you will "act" an emotion you do not feel because of your own nervousness. And the more you push the less believable your performance will become."

At this point of the session, let the children discuss moments during the presentation of a school play when they were nervous or afraid. Then end the discussion with: "I bet if you had known and used the technique of positive reaction, every one of you would have given a believable performance, regardless of the butterflies in your stomach." Next you'll introduce today's session's improvisation, the Birthday Present Buying Trip.

Divide the class into groups of four. Place a table in front of the room and tell the children that the gift items they will be working with are placed on it. "The four of you have decided to buy your friend a great gift, and since all have chipped in, you can buy something really nice."

Let each group decide on the gift they want to purchase, and continue: "Make all the imaginary things you see on the table *real*. Do you handle a T-shirt differently than a book or record? Concern yourself with the size, shape, and weight of the items you are going to handle. I want you to show delight in each and every item you examine. The first item you like a little (positive 1), the second item you like better (positive 2), but it is the third item you are really excited about (positive 3), and that's the one you are going to buy. Take time for this improvisation; don't hurry on to the really great gift, but discuss each one at length."

Beware that your group might get so caught up in the improvisation that they will disregard its purpose, the application of the three positive emotional levels. Remind them to relax, smile, and then speak.

Insist that everyone participate equally in the discussion. Make certain that the Lauras join in. Encourage your Mary Anns not to agree with everyone too readily but to offer some suggestions of their own. Encourage them to say what they want to say, and not to repeat the others' opinions.

Do not permit your Timmys to dominate the scene (this group must get over its hamming). Remind them again and again that *all* emotions should be displayed clearly and honestly.

A word of warning: Do not expect immediate results as your students work on this exercise. Have patience with them. Repeat the exercise three times if necessary before you proceed to *negative emotions.*

Explain to your group that "a negative emotion means you do not like something. This something might cause you to be angry, afraid, or sad. Whenever you dislike a thing or situation, your body will grow tense."

Ask your students to remember the imaginary-test exercise from the previous session, and how happy and relaxed they felt when the test turned out to be an easy one. "Today we will reverse the situation. Now your emotions will be negative, as you are unable to answer any questions on the test. Be aware of how tense your body grows as I talk you through the exercise.

"Ready? Here we go: Take a good look at the test. Immediately you know that you will be unable to answer *any* question. As you read the test again you become even more discouraged. You know that this test is nothing but a big, fat F. Discouraged, you hide your face in your hands."

Ask your students to experience the tension floating through them, while they remain in this position.

Then, as in the previous session, repeat counting and reciting. Have the children follow the same format they used during Session 3, only now your group's reaction will be negative:

Tense your body.
Then speak.

Repeat the Birthday Present Buying Trip. Now the purpose of the improvisation is that they do not like anything they see and decide to move on to another store.

By now the children, except maybe the Lauras, will have no difficulty expressing negative emotions.

The next exercise is an important one for the Mary Anns in your group, as they have to accept the fact that there is nothing wrong with standing up for one's opinion. One does *not* have to agree with everything another person has to say or wants one to do.

Announce the next improvisation: Going to the Movies. Divide your group into teams of two. Each team has to decide on a movie they wish to discuss. Teammate A wants to go to movie A and is all positive about it. Teammate B wants to see movie B, and is all positive about that choice. Work this improvisation in such a way that

Teammate A is *positive* about movie A and *negative* about movie B.
Teammate B is *positive* about movie B and *negative* about movie A.

Be careful that the children stick to their original positions (positive and negative). This is an improvisation you may want to repeat until all emotions are displayed clearly and precisely. Do not permit any wishy-washy performances.

Tips *to Help the Very Young Child*

The concept of bodily tension is impossible for the very young child to understand. The projection of negative emotions is especially difficult for young children, since they might remember reprimands they had been subjected to after throwing a tantrum. For this very reason, let the child know that for this session, throwing a tantrum is permitted. Have a few pillows handy and let the very small child throw them on the floor while stomping his/her foot and calling, "No—no—I don't like it."

The Birthday Present Buying Trip works well for little children if presented in a simplified form. Put three items on the table. To the first item the child responds with "I like it," and smiles; the second item he/she picks up, looks at it, and says, "I don't like it"; the third item the child pushes away angrily.

For the more mature among your very young children, you may vary this improvisation as such:

Child A likes a toy.
Child B doesn't like the toy.

Don't expect any interesting dialogue; be satisfied if the very young child communicates with "I like it" or "No, I don't like it." If you should find out that any of your group has difficulty expressing emotion, you might want to try the following exercises: 1) have the child reach for a cookie and say, "Yummy!" 2) have the child throw a pillow on the floor and yell, "No! No! No!" If in the process you find out that the children express emotions in a more volatile manner than the situation demands, do not interfere.

S E S S I O N   7

The Practice Scene

At the beginning of the session hand each student a copy of the following scene, "Advice to the New Kids."

Characters: A (Amy/Allen)
           B (Babs/Bob)
           C (Careen/Chris)
           D (Doreen/David)

Scene: *A's parents' kitchen. It is midafternoon, right after school. The editors of the famous* Woodcrest Junior High Informer *have gathered to discuss the dismal financial state of their paper.*

    A: As editor-in-chief of the *Woodcrest Junior High Informer,* it is my privilege—no, it is my duty . . .

C bursts into the room.

    C: Get off your high horse, [A], and speak like a normal human being.

26...... Teaching a Young Actor

C turns to the staff gathered around the kitchen table.

C: Sorry to be late. *(Looks around, searching for something)* Hey, got anything to eat? Like potato chips . . . a cookie or two will do.

C begins rummaging in the kitchen cupboards.

D: Forget about your stomach. Park your butt, and listen to what [A] has to say.

C: Can I help it if I'm hungry? The lunch at the cafeteria was rotten. I cannot think if I'm hungry, and . . .

B *(Interrupts):* You do have a brain? You can think?

A raps the table with a pencil.

A: Order. We are here for a serious staff meeting. Listen, [C], no one here is interested in your feeding habits. So let's get back to our discussion. . . .

D: The sad situation our newspaper is in.

C: The great, the unsurpassed *Woodcrest Junior High Informer.*

A: Don't poke fun at our paper. We have a great little newspaper. . . .

B: We *had* a great little paper. Remember, we're about to go bankrupt.

A: Well, not exactly. We still have some funds left. [B], what's in the treasury?

B searches through some papers on the table. Finally he/she takes off his/her baseball cap and pulls out a slip of paper.

B: We have two dollars and thirty cents in our treasury.

A: See, we are not broke yet *(after a moment of reflection)* . . . not exactly.

D: We have to do something—two dollars and thirty cents won't get us far.

A: That's why I have called this meeting. . . .

C's happy yell interrupts A's speech.

C: Look at this. . . .

C holds up a bag of raisins.

C: That's what I found in my coat pocket.

A glances furiously at C.

A: May I remind you that we have a meeting.

C: All right, all right, don't get huffy.

Happily, C starts eating the raisins.

A: Our school paper needs a new feature. I thought about a column for the . . . *(Dramatic pause)*

Everyone except C looks expectantly at A. C begins searching through his/her pockets.

C: I know there's another raisin . . . but where is it?

A explodes.

A: Stop your treasure hunt. Listen to what I have to say.

D *(Eagerly)*: Go on.

B: What's the new column all about?

D: Who's it for?

A: It's an advice column for kids who need help.

D: Come on . . . give.

A *(Dramatic)*: Advice to the new kids at school. We'll call it "How to Survive."

C, who was about to put a raisin in his/her mouth, drops the raisin.

B *(Weakly)*: "How to Survive"?

D: I don't know.

B: Do we know anything about how to survive at a new school?

C: We know zilch.

D: And even less about being new and alone.

B: And nothing about survival.

C: No one at Woodcrest Junior High is lonely.

A: Oh, really? How about Elsie Smith? Don't you remember how unhappy she was when Biff didn't invite her to his birthday party?

B: He didn't invite her because he didn't have a birthday party. His parents took him to Disneyland.

A *(Pushed into a corner)*: Well, if you insist on arguing with me . . .

C: [D] is not arguing, he/she is pointing out facts.

C has found more raisins. He/she throws them into the air and—head thrown back—catches them in his/her mouth.

C: And look at us, who would take advice from any of us?

A *(Knowing smile)*: No one has to know that *we* are writing the answers to the incoming letters.

C: How come?

A: Simple. We don't sign the column.

B: Have you forgotten about school rules? We have to sign *every* column.

A: All right, all right.

C *(Pressing A)*: So what do you suggest?

D: Come on . . .

B: You're the editor-in-chief.

C: You come up with an idea.

B: A bright one.

A knows that he/she's between a rock and a hard place but is determined to find a solution for the problem.

A: We sign the column "Dear Abby."

C: That's plag—plag—whatever it is.

D: That's cheating.

B: It's illegal.

C: Well, if you ask me, its a pretty neat idea.

Assign parts and give your students plenty of time to pursue the lengthy script, then announce that you will teach them some basic rules about "cold reading." A cold reading, also called a sight reading, is a reading you do not have memorized. You have, however, the responsibility to work on the script. You do this by deciding about

Positive and negative reactions and emotional levels or degrees
Intensity levels (communication levels)
Points of attention
Thought processes
Characterization
Goals

So far your group has been acquainted with positive and negative reactions, so you will stress the *application* of positives and negatives. Ask the children to memorize the script for the next session.

SESSION 8

Emotional Levels

Today your students are excited. Today they will finally perform. Before you begin the performance, explain that no one should try to impress you or the other students. "We are here to learn to clearly express emotions, to stand up for ourselves and our opinions, to use our creativity, and in the process become believable actors."

Refrain from interrupting the children as they perform. Take into consideration that most of them—except your Timmys—are nervous. Only if some of the children have failed to memorize the practice scene can you become a little more heavy-handed in your approach. Emphasize that these particular students did not fulfill their responsibilities as actors. You may add that acting—in the opinion of the British theater—is a "noble profession" that not only demands respect for anyone involved but respect for the required tasks as well.

Even if the performance is shaky at best, congratulate your students for having tried to work on their positives and negatives. Assure them that even though their performances left much to be desired, they got off to a satisfactory start.

Today's session, you will tell your group, is devoted to emotional levels, also called emotional degrees. First, make certain that your students understand what a degree or level is. Then continue: "In life we always display some feeling. We are never without any emotion. A positive emotion may be as small as the enjoyment you get from eating an ice-cream cone to the more important joy of going on a wonderful, long, planned journey, to the very, very best of everything you can imagine. And the same holds true for any negative emotion. Remember, negative emotions encompass anger, sadness, and fear. You know you may be a little angry, somewhat angry, or really furious."

Take considerable time to let the children—based on their own experiences—discuss emotional levels. Once you are sure that they are familiar with the concept, draw the following diagram on the blackboard.

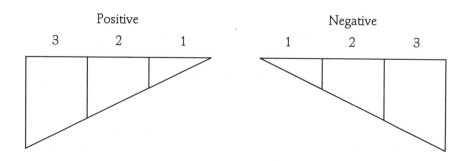

"Right now we will work on three emotional levels. As you can see on the blackboard each emotional level is listed as such":

1—low
2—medium
3—high

Positive 1—Relax, smile a little, count to ten, recite a nursery rhyme.

Positive 2—Relax, smile a much wider smile, count to ten, recite a nursery rhyme.

Positive 3—Relax, giggle and laugh, count to ten, recite a nursery rhyme.

Let the children observe that as they move up in positive degrees, their smiles become bigger. By now your group should be fully aware of the three positive emotional degrees.

Pair off the students and ask partners to tell each other a "funny story," using only numbers—no words, just numbers between one and ten and the facial expressions and gestures one uses when telling a joke or funny story. This exercise is especially helpful for the Mary Anns, who, having been delivered from the pressure of using words, can now concentrate on emotions. After this exercise has been concluded, congratulate your group on their alive and natural performances. Stress that it is not the spoken words but the displayed emotion that makes this scene come alive.

Repeat the milk commercial. Ask the children to deliver the commercial on three positive emotional levels:

Positive 1—Milk.
Positive 2—I like milk.
Positive 3—Milk is great.

Your next step will be the practice of negative emotional levels:

Negative 1—Tense your body a little, count to ten, recite a nursery rhyme.

Negative 2—Tense your stomach muscles, count to ten, recite a nursery rhyme.

Negative 3—Tense your stomach muscles, tighten your fists, count to ten, recite a nursery rhyme.

As you may have guessed, you will follow up with another partner exercise, one that again demands the projection of emotional levels by using numbers only. This exercise, however, displays three emotions:

Negative 1—Fear
        Anger
        Sadness

Negative 2—Fear
        Anger
        Sadness

Negative 3—Fear
        Anger
        Sadness

Have the children tell each other a scary story.
Have them engage in an argument.
Ask them to tell each other a sad story.

Your final exercise is the don't smoke commercial. Again, as with the milk commercial, this commercial has to be presented on three levels:

Negative 1—Cigarettes.

Negative 2—Don't smoke cigarettes.

Negative 3—Cigarettes are bad for your health.

Your students might be a little uncomfortable with the task of tensing stomach muscles and clenching fists during the negative emotional level exercise; let them know that they need these "tools" only at the beginning of their instructions. As they become more advanced, tensing won't be necessary.

Tips *to Help the Very Young Child*

I'd suggest that you stay away from any lengthy explanation but simply state, "Sometimes you like something a little, then a little better, and then a lot." Again, hand out three small pieces of candy or fruit to each child, saying, "Now eat your treat, smile a little, and say, 'I like that.' Now eat your second treat, give me a good smile, and say, 'I like that more.' Eat your third treat, smile a great big smile, and say, 'I like that best.' "

Then, as with the older children, you will repeat the milk commercial:

Smile a little and say *milk*.
Smile more and say *I like milk*.
And now a great big smile and say *milk is great*.

Remind the children of the Birthday Present Buying Trip story they acted. Show them the three items they dealt with previously: the doll, the game, and the book. Go through this exercise individually with each child, asking the child to

like the doll a little (smile a little)
like the book better (a good, medium smile)
like the game best (giggle and a great big smile)

As I have mentioned, don't expect the children to invent any lengthy dialogues; be satisfied if they express emotions strongly.

Next you'll work on negative emotional levels. Take a toy, for instance a truck, that can be taken apart easily.

Take a wheel off the truck, let the child examine the truck, and say, "Poor truck."

Take more wheels off, ask the child to clench his/her fists as hard as possible, and say, "I cannot play with my truck. . . . I cannot play with my truck."

Put all the wheels back on the truck, hand the toy back to the child, and ask him/her to take a long deep breath, smile, and say, "Now I can play with my truck."

SESSION 9

Intensity (Communication) Levels

In this session you and your students will explore *intensity* (communication) levels. On the surface intensity levels seem closely related to emotional levels, but while emotional levels pertain to the strength of the feelings projected, intensity levels pertain to levels of communication:

Intensity Level 1—You want to *explain* something.

Intensity Level 2—You want to *point out* something.

Intensity Level 3—You want to *force your opinion* upon another.

Explain the difference between emotional levels and intensity levels to your students:

Emotional Level Positive 1
I think we should go to San Diego for the weekend. It's such a fun place.

Intensity Level 1
You *explain* why a trip to San Diego should be fun.

Emotional Level Positive 2
We will see Old Town, and Coronado Island. We even may go across the border to Mexico.

Intensity Level 2
You *point out* all the great sights to see.

Emotional Level Positive 3
All right. Let's go to San Diego. Don't forget, I'm paying for this trip.

Intensity Level 3
You *force* another to accept your decision.

Take plenty of time to let your students discuss among themselves all kinds of intensity levels, be they positive or negative in nature. Before you start the Haunted House improvisation that follows (your group will love this one), make certain that your students are well aware that

Intensity levels are communication levels.

Intensity levels express the way you try to persuade someone.

Intensity levels may be either positive or negative.

Intensity levels express the intensity of your feelings.

Before you begin the Haunted House improvisation, ask your students what they know about haunted houses. Most of them will refer to the kind of haunted house some schools create for Halloween. Some of the children may have experienced the famed haunted house in Disney World or Disneyland, and—surprisingly—a number of them will talk about "real" haunted houses they have heard about or even lived in. I advise you to be *extremely careful*. Stress (whether or not this is your own belief) that ghosts exist in people's fearful minds, that the majority of hauntings can be explained as very ordinary happenings and therefore are nothing to be afraid of. Now you are ready to describe the improvisation.

"You are on vacation at a small seaside resort. You are having a wonderful time and have made friends with a great group of kids. On the outskirts of town looms an old Victorian house, which has been standing vacant for a number of years and is ready to be torn down. The roof sags, most of the windowpanes have been broken, paint peels everywhere, and the fence—supposedly protecting the old mansion—looks like a grinning toothless smile. Agreed, the house looks scary enough during the day, but at night when the moon is full, it is a truly frightening sight. There are rumors that the house is haunted.

"You and your friends have made a bet with some of the town kids. If, at the stroke of midnight, you have the courage to walk through the house from the front hall to the kitchen, you'll win a fifty-dollar prize."

After you have "cast" your students into two teams (team A and team B), go on with the story:

"Team A is happy and excited about the bet. To walk through the house will be a 'piece of cake.' You know the house is *not* haunted. Team B is afraid. They want to back out of the deal. Don't worry, we'll do the improvisation twice. Team B, the 'scaredy cats,' will have a chance to become team A, the brave ones."

Intensity level 1 takes place at the front door. Team A explains to team B why they should go through with the dare. Team B *explains* why they should not go through the house. Reluctantly, complaining about the darkness, the creaking floorboards, and the musty smell, they follow team A into the house (the classroom).

Intensity level 2 takes place in the middle of the room. Team A stops. They have discovered a shadow lurking in one of the corners. Team B *points out* that it is now time to leave; this shadow *is* a ghost. Team B is determined not to go one step farther. Team A, after exploring the strange shadow, *points out* that the shadow is nothing but an old curtain. Both teams walk on.

Intensity level 3 takes place at the window (blackboard). A member of team B screams out. Shaking, he/she points to the window (blackboard). "There it is, the ghost. Look at it." The members of team B refuse to go on. They *try to force* team A to leave immediately. "The fifty-dollar prize is not worth risking our lives for." "Team A is positive that the ghost is nothing but a tree." They *try to force* team B to go on to the kitchen.

This particular improvisation, as much fun as it is, will prove to be a difficult one for your students. Therefore, give them the opportunity to repeat the Haunted House improvisation. Whenever necessary, point out that the improvisation is a *confrontation* exercise that teaches actors to communicate with each other in ever-increasing intensity levels.

At the end of this session ask your students to memorize practice scene 2 (the second dialogue between Julie/John and Carrie/Craig).

SESSION 10

Points of Attention

Position the team as such:

Julie/John facing the camera
Carrie/Craig standing next to the camera

Explain to your students that this "setup" is called a "Reversal" in movie jargon, and instruct the student playing Julie/John to address his/her speech to the camera and *not* to the partner standing next to the camera. Point out that the camera is *not* a piece of equipment; it does *not* stand in lieu of a person; it *is* the person (Carrie/Craig) to be addressed.

In screening the tape you will notice that most children either stare at the camera or display quick and unfocused head and eye movements. Assure the children that they will have "on-camera" instructions later on. For the moment they should concentrate on an acting technique called *Points of Attention*. A Point of Attention is something or someone to look at. Go on to explain that in life—and we all know that acting at its best *does* resemble life as closely as possible—you do not look at a person all the time you are talking to him or her, but you look to the side, look down, and then back at the person.

Encourage your students to tell about something that happened to them recently and to pay close attention to *where* they look. (Do not permit any of your students to speak more than half a minute.) Next, explain Points of Attention:

Point of Attention 1—You look at and speak directly to your partner. This Point of Attention is used about 90 percent of the time.

Point of Attention 2—You look to the side. This applies to objects or people you are *talking* or *thinking* about.

Point of Attention 3—You look down. This applies when you *talk* or *think* about yourself.

Your students may say that these targets seem artificial and that they (the students) feel and look like puppets on strings. Don't worry about it; once the children are comfortable with this technique, their acting will take on a natural and easy look, and, even more important, they will feel great.

You will have fun demonstrating Points of Attention by performing a little improvisation of your own.

LINES	POINT OF ATTENTION
Children, let's stop everything for a moment. You know what—I was just thinking—where are my car keys?	Point of Attention 1, "other person"—look at your students
I know I . . .	Point of Attention 3, "myself"—look down

LINES	POINT OF ATTENTION
Locked my car . . .	Point of Attention 1, "other person"—look at your students
Walked across the parking lot . . .	Point of Attention 2, "what is spoken about"—look to the side
To my classroom (stage) I know I put my keys into my purse . . .	Point of Attention 1, "other person"—look at your students
But where are they?	Point of Attention 3—start searching through your purse

Without a doubt, all of your students will rush to the door, eager to search the parking lot for your missing keys. Explain that you were performing for them, then tell them about the first improvisation for today's session: Lost in a Strange City.

This improvisation requires two players. The object is to teach the actors to target the objects discussed, as well as his or her partner. This is the story:

"Your parents have taken you to Paris. You are staying at the Ritz hotel. Your parents have a business meeting and, to get you out of their hair, have suggested you do some sightseeing. They told you to be back at the hotel at noon.

"You pass by a fantastic window display [the blackboard], admire the items in it (Point of Attention 2), and discuss these items with your partner (Point of Attention 1). Then you decide it is time to go back to the hotel. But where is the hotel? You have forgotten its location."

One partner points to one corner of the room (Point of Attention 2): "I know we came by the Eiffel Tower"; the other contends that he/she saw the Cathedral of Notre Dame (Point of Attention 2) from the dining-room window. Partners talk to each other (Point of Attention 1) and argue about what way to take back to the hotel.

The next improvisation, The Spy at the Airport, demands acting techniques of Points of Attention and intensity levels.

CHARACTERS: Spy
Owner of souvenir booth
Happy Traveler 1
Happy Traveler 2

PROPS: Table on which a number of newspapers and magazines are displayed.

The spy's magazine.

Blackboard (the booth) on which several items (teddy bear, T-shirt, candy, bottles of perfume) are drawn.

Two chairs (waiting area) for the happy travelers.

Story:

This improvisation takes place at an international airport. A spy enters. He/she carries a magazine that contains a coded message. The spy is supposed to drop the magazine at a spot where another spy will pick it up. The spy walks up to the souvenir booth and asks to be shown one of the items on the blackboard. As soon as the owner of the booth turns his/her back, the spy places the coded magazine among the other magazines on the table. He/she may or may not buy the item he/she asked to see.

Two happy travelers are sitting in the waiting area. Since the flight to New York will be a long one and they are tired of watching in-flight movies, they decide to buy some magazines. They walk up to the souvenir stand. Trying to decide which magazines they wish to buy, they divide their Points of Attention between the magazines and each other. The spy's task is to watch the happy travelers *and* the magazines. His/her Points of Attention are divided between the happy travelers and the magazines.

Tips *to Help the Very Young Child*

Points of Attention, as well as the exercises leading to the confident application of this technique, are too involved for the very young child. But the Visit to the Zoo improvisation should teach this concept to your young students. It is helpful if the children have been to a zoo and have seen some of the animals.

The improvisation should be done individually. If you are teaching a larger group it might be a good idea to ask some older students to volunteer. They will like it.

Take the very young child by the hand and say: "Let's make believe that you and I are at the zoo. Now we are looking at the monkeys. Remember how funny they looked swinging from tree to tree, and how neatly one peeled a banana? You and I will look at the monkeys—make believe they are right there"—point to some chairs, the cages—"and then when we talk to each other about the monkeys you'll look at me."

Some young children will respond well to this exercise; others might be confused, because there are no monkeys. If this is the case, place a few stuffed animals on the chairs.

S E S S I O N   1 1

Thoughts

Show a clip of a movie or TV show that demonstrates the way good actors *think*. Thoughts are the elements still missing in your students' performances. Tell your students that a thought may be placed

> before a line
> in the middle of a line
> after a line

As you show the film clip a second time, remark how clearly actors show their feelings through thoughts. This, however, means that the actor should not simply *pause* while speaking lines but should think real thoughts. To practice this technique, ask your students each to pick a sentence from their practice script 1. Make them aware that

> Thoughts, like spoken lines, have to have a Point of Attention.
> Thoughts, like spoken lines, can be positive or negative.

Sample sentence: "Nothing can be perfect. I've told you so a thousand times."

> *Thought before a line*: "What a dumb bunny."
> *Point of Attention*: 2, Side (what is thought about)

Spoken line: "Nothing can be perfect. I've told you so a thousand times."
Points of Attention: 1, other person
Thought: Positive
Spoken line: Positive

Thought in the middle of a line
Spoken line: "Nothing can be perfect."
Point of Attention: 1, other person
Thought: I have to help my friend.
Point of Attention: 3, myself
Spoken lines: "I've told you so a thousand times."
Thought and spoken lines: Positive

Thought after a line
Spoken lines: "Nothing can be perfect. I've told you so a thousand times."
Thought: "I have to help my friend."
Point of Attention: 1, other person
Thought and spoken lines: Positive

From there you'll proceed to the Angry Customer improvisation.

CHARACTERS: Cashier
Bagger
Customer without ID
Angry Customer

PROPS: Table that serves as checkout counter
Chair that serves as shopping basket
Pencil, library card, ID card, newspaper clipping

Story:

The story takes place at the checkout counter of a supermarket. A customer who wants to pay for several items with a check has no ID. During a lengthy search for his/her driver's license, the customer pulls out first a library card, then the membership card of a health club, and finally a newspaper clipping showing him/her with a prize-winning cat. The angry customer behind, wanting to pay for only a pencil, watches the proceedings with increasing impatience.

Tasks:

Bagger has to make the imaginary items real (a bag of potatoes is heavier than a cereal box). Eggs need to be handled more carefully than a bag of flour or sugar.

Cashier and customer without ID have to work on increasing intensity levels, as the customer insists that his/her ID ought to be accepted, and the cashier contends he/she can't.

Angry customer must show *silently* what he/she thinks and feels about the delay. The actor works on Points of Attention and thoughts, as well as on intensity levels, as he/she shows increasing frustration.

S E S S I O N   1 2

Characterization

Characterization means you show the audience a character's basic *personality* and *behavioral pattern*. People come in all sizes and shapes, and they have all kinds of personalities: Some people are giving and considerate, others are selfish; some are timid and others are aggressive; some are down to earth and other are conceited. Ask your students to talk about personalities they know. Later explain that as one portrays a character on stage or screen, one must not only be familiar with this character's personality but also make it visible to the audience via characterization. Characterization includes a person's behavior, moods, way of speech, movement, and attire. Characterization also takes into account age and educational and social background. Touch upon these areas briefly, as most of your students won't be mature enough to deal with these concepts in depth.

Ask your students to characterize the characters of their practice scene 3 (pages 25–29). Your students should come up with all kinds of different characterizations; take Chris/Careen, for instance:

I want the audience to admire Chris/Careen. He/she has fun and takes nothing seriously.

or

I want the audience to find Chris/Careen obnoxious. He/she is selfish and the most ineffective member of the staff.

or

I want my audience to think Chris/Careen is really funny. He/she is a clown that keeps people off balance. Regardless of Chris/Careen's actions, everyone likes him/her.

Permit your students to improvise on practice scene 3 by paraphrasing the lines and by concentrating on characterizing their respective characters. This exercise will teach your students that *depending on different actors' characterizations, the audience will perceive a character in different ways, regardless of the lines.*

Your group will enjoy creating different characterizations for these fairy-tale characters.

Snow White (*The wicked stepmother [peddler] offers her the poisoned apple.*)
    Snow White is shy and submissive.
    Snow White bargains with the peddler (she is stingy).
    Snow White tells the peddler her wares are rotten.
    Snow White gives the peddler a lecture on sales techniques (she is
        conceited).
Jack* (*Jack meets the giant.*)
    Jack is afraid of the giant.
    Jack is conceited.
    Jack is mildly interested in the giant.
    Jack is a Hollywood agent who tries to get the giant as a client.
Cinderella (*Cinderella asks to be taken to the ball.*)
    Cinderella is afraid of her stepmother.
    The stepmother wants to take her to the ball, but Cinderella is more
        interested in redecorating the house.
    Cinderella doesn't think much of royalty and makes fun of the
        stepmother's desire to meet Prince Charming.

*from "Jack and the Beanstalk"

Tips *to Help the Very Young Child*

All of the fairy tales in the previous exercise, in a very simplified form, make fun improvisations for the very young child.

S E S S I O N   1 3

Think on Your Feet

This particular session has been designed to gauge the progress your Mary Anns and Lauras have made. By now they should be able, at least to some degree, to stand up for themselves and to make their opinions known.

CHARACTERS: Judge
                Prosecutor
                Plaintiff
                Defense Attorney
                Defendant
                Witnesses for both parties

PROPS: Table and chair for the judge
           Chair (witness stand)
           Chairs for the rest of the cast

Story:

    The improvisation takes place in a courtroom. A necklace that once belonged to the Empress Josephine of France has been chosen for an antique jewelry exhibit. The planned exhibit, and especially the necklace, have received much media coverage. The necklace, at the time of an alleged burglary, was kept in the owner's residence in Beverly Hills. On Halloween the owner had some roof repair done. Due to impending rain the roofers did not complete the job but placed canvas over the opening in the roof and left a ladder—expecting to return the next day—leaning against the house. The owner left to attend a party in Santa Barbara. On Halloween night a person dressed in a black outfit, with a belt containing some burglary tools around his/her waist, climbed onto the roof, fell through the opening, and landed in the living room, breaking his/her leg. In due course this person sued the owner for negligence.

The plaintiff's story: The plaintiff was invited to a Halloween party. Since a prize for the most authentic costume was promised, the plaintiff rented an authentic burglary outfit from a costume shop. To make things even more real he/she purchased tools that could be used in a burglary. On the way to the party, the plaintiff's car ran out of gas. Since the Beverly Hills residential area has only a few service stations, the plaintiff decided to ask one of the homeowners for help. The plaintiff parked his/her car and went to a house where he saw lights. On his/her way the plaintiff was attacked by a Great Dane. To his/her relief the plaintiff saw a ladder leaning against a house. He/she ran to the ladder, climbed to the roof, and consequently fell through the opening.

The defendant's story: The defendant did have some roof repair done. On Halloween morning he/she left to visit some friends and to attend a Halloween party. The defendant had asked his/her neighbor to watch the house. The neighbor noticed a car stopping in front of the defendant's house, put his/her Great Dane on a leash, and went outside to inquire. The neighbor saw a person climbing the ladder leaning against the house. Confident that this person was a burglar, the neighbor let the dog off the leash.

There is no predictable outcome to this story; it all depends on the witnesses' testimony. Basically the trial hinges on two questions:

Did the dog chase the plaintiff?
Was the plaintiff on the ladder before the dog chased him/her?

Before attempting this improvisation, discuss with your students the rudiments of court procedure:

Attorneys' opening statements
Witnesses' examination and cross-examination
Attorneys' right to object
Judge's responsibility to sustain or overrule the objection.

Watch your students and have fun. You will be amazed by their logic and vitality.

Tips *to Help the Very Young Child*

This session for younger children deals with *memorization* and *characterization*.

Repeat a nursery rhyme. First speak a line that the children repeat in unison. Then, work with them on the rudiments of memorization. I've found the combination of actual physical action and voice repetition very helpful for children between the ages of three and five. The technique works as such:

Jimmy, please walk over to the table and say: "I'll walk over to the table." (The child does the combination of physical and verbal action.)

Pick up a pencil and say: "I pick up a pencil." (The child does the combination of physical and verbal action.)

Now take the pencil over to the chair, and say: "I'll take the pencil over to the chair." (The child does the combination of physical and verbal action.)

Bring me the pencil, please, and say: "Here is the pencil, Teacher." (The child does the combination of physical and verbal action.)

Insist that the children repeat *verbatim* what you ask them to do. Do not permit them to substitute words or phrases of their own. Production companies making commercials demand that the commercial actor, regardless of age, speak the copy word for word. After all, the copy has been approved by the ad agency and, even more important, by the sponsor whose product the commercial advertises. Believe me, any deviation from the approved text is considered sacrilege.

As soon as the students are familiar with the lines and physical actions, require them to repeat the sequence without your coaching:

Physical Action	*Verbal Action*
Walks to table	I'll walk over to the table.
Picks up pencil	I'll pick up the pencil.

Physical Action	Verbal Action
Takes pencil to a chair	I'll take the pencil over to the chair.
Takes pencil to teacher	Here is the pencil, Teacher.

Finally, you'll add *characterization* to the sequence. Keep the verbal and physical actions as practiced before, but ask your students to add these "feelings":

Smile and have lot of fun carrying the pencil around.

Now you are very much afraid of the pencil. You are afraid it might bite you.

Imagine that the pencil is a soft, tiny kitten. Touch the kitten very carefully. Show how much you love it.

These exercises are fairly easy to do. They are fun for the children and are important instructional tools as well. The very small child who wants to work in the industry has to become comfortable with physical actions, the projection of emotions, and the memorization of short lines.

Additional Exercises and Short Scenes for Very Young Children

The following are exercises and short scenes for little children. Each of them may be incorporated in any of the previous segments.

TRAIN
(Kinesthetic Exercise)

Place the children in a line: One is the train's engine, several are the cars, one is the caboose. Place chairs (the train stations) in various areas of the room. Now, as the children hold on to one another, have the train proceed—on straight tracks, around curves, up an incline, and down another one. Have the train speed up and slow down; have it stop at the train stations.

TOYS IN A TOY STORE
(Physical and Verbal Expression)

Characters: Doll
Ball
Truck
Airplane
Cat
Clown puppet

Scene:

It is the day before Christmas, and all the toys are eagerly waiting to be bought.

DOLL: I know someone will buy me for a sweet little girl. I will look beautiful under the Christmas tree.

Showing off her fancy dress, the doll parades by the other toys, twirls around, and smiles prettily.

BALL: And I will be given to a boy. I will bounce up and down.

Bounces up and down, right and left.

TRUCK: My new owner can load lots of things on me, and then I'll take off— *Grrrrrr*—down the road.

Yelling Grrrrrrrrrr, *the truck moves around the room; all toys run to the side.*

AIRPLANE: But I'll fly in the air. I'll be so much faster than you, little truck.

Arms stretched to the side, the airplane runs in a straight line (the runway), then takes off and "flies" in circles around the room.

CAT: Meow, meow, meow. I want to go to a child who will love and cuddle me. My fur is so soft, I'm so playful. . . .

The cat rolls over on the floor, then chases an (imaginary) ball of yarn.

CLOWN PUPPET: Look at me, look at me, I can dance, I can jump. I have lots of fun. Buy me, buy me.

Movements jerky, but happy, the clown dances over to the doll, bows in front of her. The doll curtsies.

ALL TOGETHER: Tomorrow is Christmas and we will find wonderful homes.

It is the day after Christmas, and none of the toys has found a home.

DOLL: I don't have a little girl to love me.

Dejectedly the doll walks around and finally flops down on the floor.

BALL: I cannot even bounce any longer.

Tries to bounce, but hardly gets off the floor; flops down next to the doll.

TRUCK: And I cannot get my engine started. Listen to that Gr—Gr—Gr—Gr.

Stands stiffly.

AIRPLANE: I cannot get off the ground.

Crumbles on the floor.

CAT: Meow, meow. I have no one to cuddle me, to play with me. I'm a sad kitten. I cannot even catch my ball of yarn.

Tries to catch the ball of yarn and fails.

CLOWN: I . . . cannot . . . dance . . . anymore.

The clown tries to lift an arm, then a leg, his/her movements becoming slower and slower and finally stopping.

ALL TOGETHER: We all are sad toys.

It is not necessary for the children to memorize the lines; let them express their emotions any way they want to, but pay attention that both movement and speech express identical emotions (either happy or sad).

FLOWERS IN A MEADOW
(Kinesthetic Exercise)

Explain to the children that they are flowers in a meadow. Ask them to act out the story you are going to tell them:

It is early morning; your pedals are closed. (Close your arms over your heads.)

The sun comes up and slowly, slowly you wake up. Open your petals [arms], lift your face to the sun, enjoy the sunshine.

And now a slight wind comes up; move with the wind back and forth.

The wind becomes stronger and stronger; move along with it.

And now rain pours down—quickly protect yourself by closing your petals. (Arms over your head.)

But now the sun comes up again; happily you lift your face toward it.

CLOUDS
(Kinesthetic Exercise)

Characters: Sunshine
              Wind
              Several Clouds

Happily the clouds drift along.

After a while the wind begins to chase the clouds. First the clouds enjoy the game, but as the wind turns into a storm, they become angry and afraid.

Finally the sun rises up behind the clouds and chases the wind away.

DAY IN THE WOODS
(Physical and Verbal Expression)

Characters: Leader
　　　　　　Several Hikers

Ask your kids to improvise the dialogue as they express their emotions physically. This exercise acquaints your students with the way they feel physically during different times of the day.

Leader arranges the hikers in a group. All hikers carry imaginary knapsacks.

Happily they begin their hike in the woods. The leader asks them to
　Enjoy walking
　Enjoy the fresh morning air
　Enjoy the sunshine

Hiker 1 becomes tired; the knapsack is too heavy for him/her. The hiker begins to complain.

Leader asks the hikers to follow these instructions:
　Now we walk slower, because we walk uphill.
　We stop to look at a squirrel running up a tree. Look up, up, up.

Hiker 2 stops and takes off a sweater and complains that he/she is thirsty.

Leader warns the hikers:
　Walk slowly and carefully; we are going down a steep incline. Hold
　on to one another's hands.

Hiker 3 walks slowly, complaining that his/her foot hurts. Hiker 3 stops to take off his/her shoes and finds a pebble.

Leader tells the children that they have arrived at their destination. The hikers plop down exhausted on the ground. Leader advises:
　Take out your (imaginary) sandwiches and soft drinks.

After the hikers enjoy their lunch, they lie down to rest.

WE FEEL AND MOVE DIFFERENTLY IN VARIOUS OUTFITS
(Physical Expression)

Ask your students to express the way they feel *without* using words, but simply by the way they *move*.

> You wear your *very best* outfit. You have to be very careful not to get it dirty or wrinkled.

> You wear your everyday "grubbies." You are very comfortable.

> Your shoes are new and pinch.
> Your shoes are too tight.

> Your coat pinches under your arms.

> You wear an outfit that fits well, but you cannot stand the look of it.

> You wear an outfit you always wanted.

HALLOWEEN CHARACTERS
(Physical Expression)

Ask the children to move as if they were

> A clown
> A princess
> Batman
> A Ninja Turtle

PART TWO

On-camera Techniques

Close-up

So far students have learned to express themselves clearly and honestly. They have become more assertive and, we hope, are more in tune with the wide range of emotion at their disposal. Now they are anxious to "show off" what they have learned and eager to gauge their progress. The time has come to devote some sessions to *on-camera technique.*

It is my firm belief that every actor, regardless of age, ought to be familiar with on-camera technique and must be relaxed in front of the camera. It is not uncommon for actors who have been cast for their vitality and acting ability to fail miserably on the set.

Many actors, untrained in on-camera technique and overwhelmed by the technical demands (hitting marks, playing to the camera, taking the correct angle, avoiding quick head and eye movements, etc.), fail to function effectively and bring in either a static or an "acty" performance.

These are the areas you and your group will be dealing with during the following sessions:

Close-up
Standing and/or Seated Two-shot
Walking Two-shot
Reversals
Basic Shots
Marks

Chances are that you, the instructor, are neither an actor nor a director and that the idea of incorporating camera terminology and techniques may seem a little intimidating at first. Don't worry, once you've got the hang of it, on-camera techniques are fairly easy to teach.

While watching TV or a movie, familiarize yourself with the previously mentioned camera moves and angles. You do not need any complicated equipment to teach on-camera techniques; a video camera will do just fine. As your students begin to enjoy their "movie" performances, be careful that they respect each other's work and try not to overshadow a partner. There are some tricks even professional actors use to overshadow a partner:

Blocking a partner by leaning too far in
Arbitrary head or hand movements in a Two-shot
The use of props to draw attention away from the partner
Not listening while a partner speaks

(By the way, the on-camera technique you will be teaching during the next few sessions is, if simplified, equally effective for the very young child.)

First, let your students "make friends with the camera." Make certain they understand this concept:

The camera is not some kind of equipment.
It does not stand in lieu of a person.
The camera is a person.

Again, as during the first session of Part 1, let each of your students tell a story. Only this time the children will talk to their camera-friend. Expect to see unprofessional performances on the screen: Head movements may be too quick, and eye movements may be unmotivated. Therefore, I suggest that you review the basic Points of Attention:

Other person (look at camera)
What is thought or spoken about (look to the side)
Myself (look down)

After this review ask your students to repeat their on-camera performance while observing Points of Attention. Make your students aware that all

movements performed in front of a camera have to be slowed down somewhat. This holds true for body as well as head and eye movements.

Set your camera up for a close-up. A close-up shows the actor's head
and shoulders. In a close-up it is especially important that an actor's head
and eye movements are controlled but natural. Don't permit

Overacting (grimacing)
Excessive head and eye movements
Dull or static expressions

After your group has gained some confidence, ask them to

Be angry with the camera-friend
Ask the camera-friend to do a favor
Tell the camera-friend a secret
Explain something to the camera-friend

Be angry with the camera-friend.
I don't like spinach; I told you a million times I don't like spinach.

Ask the camera-friend to do a favor.
Please help me clean up my room. Please, Please.

Tell the camera-friend a secret.
I know a secret. A really big secret. Want to hear? Mom and Dad are
going to take us to visit Grandma in Denver!

Explain something to the camera-friend.
All right, just listen up. I want you to go to the supermarket to buy a
few groceries. Here is the list: I need eggs, butter, and bread.

Remind your group that on-screen the actors use two Points of Attention—*myself* and *what is thought or spoken about*:

During his/her lines
While listening to his/her partner's lines

The *other person* Point of Attention is usually directed to the partner during either the actor's or partner's lines.

This is an example of how Points of Attention work:

Other person	Guess what? Yesterday Bill . . .
Myself	and I . . .
What is thought or spoken about	went to the animal shelter . . .
Other person	to adopt a cat.

At the end of this session, hand out the following practice scene. Cast the scene and emphasize that the lines *must* be memorized, since the practice scene is the backbone for all ensuing "on-camera" sessions.

This practice scene is called "The New Kid on the Block."

Characters: A (Ann/Allen)
B (Barbara/Bill)
Mother's Voice

> Scene: *The front veranda of a Victorian house. Late afternoon. A, sitting on the front stoop, looks at the yard. The movers have left only a short while ago. The yard is littered with packing material and empty boxes.*
>
> *B, a pleasant-looking youngster, walks by.*

B: Hi, I'm [Barbara/Bill]. You just moved in?

A: Right. Hi, I'm [Ann/Allen].

They look at each other; there is an uneasy pause. Then A motions to the stairs.

A: Why don't you sit down?

B sits down next to A.

B: Thanks.

B points to another Victorian house across the street.

B: I live over there with my parents and my pesky little brother. And I go to Midvale [Elementary/Junior High].

A: That's where I'm going to go. Do you like Midvale?

B: Yeah, it's a neat place. The teachers—some of them—are really strict, but they're fair. And we have a great athletic department. Do you play tennis?

A: I never tried it. I'm more into drama.

B: Really?

A: Yes, we put on a lot of plays at Sequoia [Elementary/Junior High]; it's in Fresno.

B: That's where you moved from?

A: Yes. And we were going to do "Cinderella." I was cast as Lucifer the cat, but then Dad was transferred and . . . we moved.

B: I can tell you are sorry to have missed out on that one.

A nods.

B: I don't think we have a drama club at Midvale, but we have a community theater *(A smiles an assuring smile),* and they always put on kids' shows for the holidays. My homeroom teacher, Mrs. McDowney, is a member; maybe—

A: Mrs. McDowney, you said? She's my homeroom teacher, too.

B: Hey, we're classmates. I like that.

A: I like that, too.

MOTHER'S VOICE: [B], come on home, you still have to do the dishes.

B: Yes, Mother. I'll be right there.

B turns to A.

B: I've got to run. Chores to do. Do you want me to pick you up tomorrow morning? We can walk to school together.

A: Thank you. That would be nice.

Tips *to Help the Very Young Child*

All of the camera techniques listed above are suitable for very young children. To make "line reading" easier for this particular group, you might speak a line first and then have the children repeat it. Most likely none of your group will have any problem memorizing the text. It may be necessary at times that you speak one line, have the child repeat it, and then tape the child.

S E S S I O N 2

Standing and/or Seated Two-shot

Today you will be working on a Two-shot. A Two-shot shows two actors either sitting, standing, or walking side by side. Normally in this position two people will face each other in such a way as to be seen in profile. The static line of nose and chin, however, gives little opportunity to show expression. Only eyes and mouth show feelings. For this reason the actor will choose what is called a *45-degree-angle head position,* a position that shows eyes and mouth at least partially. If we consider that a head motion ranging from chest to shoulder has a 90-degree angle, then the half-point position provides the desired 45-degree angle. This angle is the *other person* Point of Attention—the actor's partner. This particular Point of Attention, of course, does not permit the actors to look at each other. Two actors seated (or standing) next to each other will *not* be able to gauge each other's expressions and reactions. At first, conversing in such a way seems strange to actors unaccustomed to on-camera techniques. After a while, however, actors will feel completely at ease.

Next you'll work on "loosening up" the Two-shot; that is, do not permit the children to "get stuck" on the *other person* Point of Attention. In life, we do not always look at the person we are talking to; at times we look down or to the side in the very same way your students practiced during the close-up.

Most important, do not pressure any child to do the Two-shot. Admittedly, the Two-shot poses problems to many adult acting students. Tell your students, "I know the Two-shot poses a big hurdle for you. If you feel very uncomfortable, let's forget the Two-shot for the moment." After a few weeks, or possibly months, go back to this difficult but important on-camera technique. You, the teacher, must not take the *fun* out of the acting classes. Never give your students any reason to fear that they cannot do it.

S E S S I O N   3

Walking Two-shot

If your students had difficulties comprehending the standing and seated Two-shot, I strongly suggest that you postpone the walking Two-shot.

Start this session out by repeating the standing or seated Two-shot. Utilize the appropriate practice scenes for this purpose, and mention again the importance of Points of Attention. By now your students should be familiar with the Two-shot. Explain to them that the next step they have to take (literally)—the walking Two-shot—sounds complicated but is fairly easy to do, if they observe the following rules:

Walk closely (almost shoulder to shoulder). Remain side by side. No actor should lag behind or walk ahead of the other actor.

Watch your marks. (We will discuss marks later.) When the director calls "action":

Do not begin walking immediately but wait for two beats (count silently—one thousand and one, one thousand and two).

Do not walk and talk simultaneously but speak one or two words before you commence your walk.

Both partners *must begin walking at the same time*. As in the seated or standing Two-shot, actors must maintain a 45-degree angle as they look at each other.

Move smoothly into the Reversal. (We will discuss Reversals in the next session.) Do not pull away from each other as you turn to face each other; remain close.

When stepping out of your Reversal, back into the Two-shot; step out on the foot that *faces* the camera.

Permit your students to rehearse several times before you tape the scene. The children will be surprised how easy the "scary" walking Two-shot really is, and you will be delighted that all of a sudden your students' performances have taken on an almost professional flair.

S E S S I O N   4

Reversal

Whenever actors are in opposite positions facing each other, they are in a *Reversal.* One kind of Reversal is when an actor has been placed in front of the camera and the partner has been positioned next to the camera.

For the actor facing the camera, obviously, the camera *is* the partner.

Another kind of Reversal takes place when, during a walking Two-shot, actors stop and turn to face each other. They will *not* direct their lines to each other's eyes (as onstage) but to the partner's ear that faces the camera. Again, as in the Two-shot, actors have to recognize that they are unable to gauge the partner's reaction.

And this brings us to the *Reaction Shot.* A Reaction Shot takes place when the camera focuses on the actor who *listens,* while his/her partner speaks. Remind your students to observe the following:

Do not stare at a hole in space; think real thoughts. Your response to your partner's lines will be the result of these thoughts.

Remember that thoughts, like spoken words, are based on negatives and positives as well as on Points of Attention.

Pause for two beats (count silently one thousand and one, one thousand and two) before you answer your partner. (Explain to your students that this lapse is needed to edit the Reversal effectively.)

To practice the actor's response in a Reversal you may want to utilize two practice scenes such as "The New Kid on the Block" or "Snow White and the Peddler."

Tips *to Help the Very Young Child*

When working on reactions with the very young child, place the child in front of the camera, and while you stand next to the camera, do the following:

Hand the child a cuddly animal or doll and say: "Love the dolly/kitten. Cuddle it. Show me how much you love it."

Show the child a little birthday cake and say: "Nod and smile when I ask you whether you like the cake."

Show the child a plate and say: "Imagine there is something on this plate you really do not like to eat. Shake your head and shudder a little."

SESSION 5

The Basic Shots

This session is a fun one. By now your students have gained confidence and will have no problem when you introduce them to the following basic shots:

Medium Shot   (down to waist)
Three-quarter Shot (down to knees)
Full Shot   (down to feet)
Pan Shot
Walk-in Shot

Place each student in front of the camera and have him or her repeat the following lines (or some lines of their own choice) in close-up, medium shot, three-quarter shot, and full shot:

Today is the first day of school.
I look forward to it.
I'll see my friends again, and I'll learn new things.
Yes, I'm looking forward to school this year.

As your students watch the tape they will discover that facial expressions and head movements have to be far less animated in close-up and medium shots than in three-quarter or full shots.

Lines: I'll have to go to the library before it closes. (Pan Shot)
Lines: Did you see Aunt Alice? (Walk-in Shot)

Pan Shot. The actor crosses as the camera pans with him or her. (If you, the instructor, operate the camera, watch that the camera *leads*, not *follows*, the actor.)
Walk-in Shot. Position actor A in front of the camera, and have him or her speak lines while actor B enters the shot from off-camera.

SESSION 6

Marks

It is now about time to teach *marks* to your students. Marks are the *exact spots where an actor has to stop* during shooting. Your students have to learn to deal with two kinds of marks:

Floor marks
Peripheral marks

Floor Marks. These are chalk marks or taped marks on the floor:

X marks
T marks
Line marks

It is the actor's responsibility to hit the mark exactly—that is, the actor's foot must be right on the mark, not a few inches above or below it.

Peripheral Marks. These are items (usually furniture, trees, architectural props) that the actor can see out of the corner of his or her eyes. A peripheral mark indicates that the actor either stops or commences moving as soon as he or she is in line with the designated object.

Dealing effectively with marks is one of the responsibilities of the skilled motion picture actor.

Have your students hit the listed floor mark during the following short monologue:

(Walk) I have looked all through the house . . .

(Stop at X mark) but I could not find the book.

(Walk) Maybe . . .

(Stop at T mark) I've lost it.

(Walk) No, I know I've got it somewhere.

(Stop at line mark) What do you think?

Next, work with your students on peripheral marks as they speak their monologue:

(Walk) I better get my suitcase packed.

(Stop at chair) Almost forgot to pick up the dry cleaning.

(Walk) And I should get my surfboard.

(Stop at table) Too bad I let Becky borrow it.

Tips *to Help the Very Young Child*

Contrary to common belief, hitting marks does not pose any problem to the very young child, if you keep the lines the little ones have to speak easy enough. Since TV, movies, and commercials do require strict adherence to marks, these ought to be practiced with the very young group. Just make these exercises fun to do.

I suggest that as you rehearse floor marks you restrict your little ones to physical actions *only,* and have props handy.

(Walk)

(Stop at the X mark, bend down, and pick up a flower)

(Walk)

(Stop at the T mark, pick up a basket, and put the flowers into the basket)

For peripheral marks, either repeat the above-listed physical actions or have your students say some simple lines.

(Walk)

(Stop at a chair) I'm going on vacation.

(Walk) I'm going to the beach.

(Stop at a table) I'll have lots of fun.

PART THREE

Thinking Skills: Nonverbal Acting Techniques

So far your students have learned to express their emotions using verbal acting techniques. In this section they will be introduced to aspects of nonverbal acting:

Making physical contact with one another.
Listening to one another (not so much the spoken words as the *inflection* of the words).
Becoming fully involved in thoughts that lead to emotions, verbal expression, and physical actions.

Verbal acting places primary importance upon the *word,* and at times either hides or controls actual emotion, whereas in nonverbal acting the prime importance is placed on the actor's impulses (thoughts, feelings, and physical acting) that lead to words.
In other words:

In verbal acting, words are the springboard for the actor's emotions.
In nonverbal acting, impulses (thoughts, feelings, and physical actions) lead to words.

S E S S I O N   1

Permit Yourself to Think

Begin this session with a story-telling segment. Ask your students to concentrate on the emotions they encounter before they speak. At this time it might be a good idea to introduce your group to the detailed emotional sequence that precedes verbal expression.

> *Motive* (an incident that causes a response): A mouse runs over your foot, which leads to
> *Physical sensation*: Knot in your stomach, which leads to
> *Thought*: A rat, which leads to
> *Physical action*: You jump away, which leads to
> *Verbal expression:* Scream.

Do not hesitate to interrupt your students whenever you feel that their verbal expression is taking precedence over their thoughts and feelings. Granted, some children do not take easily to your request to "think and feel," so you might help them by asking

> What did you feel?
> Tell me what you thought at this moment.
> How did your body feel? Was your throat restricted? Did you have a knot in your stomach? Were you happy enough to jump around?

Do not let the children get off easily. Dig for answers. At this point I suggest that you tell your group about the techniques of *method acting*, which deals with the exploration of the senses, such as smell, sound, sight, taste, and touch. These techniques will be dealt with extensively in Part 4 of this book. For now, your students should be introduced to the immense value of method acting, as in the following example:

> Student: I went to a really neat party and I wore this dress. I picked it out all by myself and bought it with my own money—the money I saved from baby-sitting.

Do not accept this story, but start digging for the sensory aspects of it. After all, the way senses respond to *motives* changes emotions and thoughts.

YOU: Tell me more about that wonderful dress.

STUDENT: It's pink.

YOU: What kind of pink?

STUDENT (*Reflects*): Soft pink . . . like . . . like . . . you see, my grandmother has a garden and she has these roses . . . yes, soft pink like my grandmother's roses.

YOU: Now touch this wonderful pink dress.

STUDENT: How can I? I don't have the dress here.

YOU: Imagine the dress hanging in front of you. Look at it; now touch it with your fingertips. How does the fabric feel?

STUDENT: Kind of silky—no, no—slick and stiff—satin.

YOU: Can you smell something?

STUDENT: Oh, yes. Mom let me have some of her perfume.

YOU: Try to remember what you thought when you put the dress on.

STUDENT: Do I have to tell?

YOU: Not if you don't want to.

STUDENT (*Hesitates*): I thought I was a movie star, or maybe Cinderella.

YOU: What did you feel?

Student, spreading her arms, weaves slightly to and fro. There is a big happy smile on her face:

STUDENT: I felt like floating away on a cloud.

Next, let your students enjoy a movie sequence that shows actors observing and thinking, and discuss with your students the thoughts and emotions they witnessed on the screen. Conclude today's session with the Boring Conversation improvisation.

Ask the children to remember a family reunion or any other gathering where they had to listen to much boring talk. (There is, of course, no actual conversation for them to react to.) Each of your students will have to make up the conversation in his or her mind. Provide your group with a few scattered chairs to use for Points of Attention, and ask them to verbalize their thoughts. Such verbalization may run something like this:

Why do I have to listen to this? I would much rather spend the afternoon outdoors, playing tennis, swimming, shopping. And here I have to listen for the millionth time to Uncle John's boring college stories . . . and, oh no, here we go again—cousin Ida is handing little Jennifer's— the monster's—baby pictures around.

Tips *to Help the Very Young Child*

The concept of "permitting yourself to think" is far too complex for very young children. Still, they have to learn how to think on stage and screen. Explain: "When you speak, often it is to say that you like something or that you don't like something. Well, when you think, the same thing happens. Some of your thoughts—like your words—are happy; some are sad or angry."

Hold up a glass and say, "Look, here I have a glass filled with water."

Hand the glass to one of the children and ask: "Can you imagine this is not water but some yucky medicine you'll have to take? Now hold the glass, look at the water, and think: 'I don't want to take this medicine. It tastes bitter. It tastes bad.' "

Give the child some time to absorb and act upon your demand before you continue: "Look at the medicine once more and say, 'I don't like it.' "

Next, reward your very young students with the Birthday Cake improvisation. Have a little cake ready, show it to the children, and say: "Isn't this a nice birthday cake? Look how pretty it is. Do you think it tastes yummy? Look at it, and think how good it will taste, then say: 'I like that cake.' "

S E S S I O N   2

Talking to Yourself (Monologue)

Start this session by explaining the term *monologue*. When a character talks to himself or herself we call it a monologue. On the surface, such a string of uninterrupted words seems to be an artificial way of expressing one's emotion. Remind your group that this is not necessarily so; at times we *do* talk to ourselves. Mostly people talk to themselves when they are under stress. This is why the words of a monologue are not as important as the reason a character speaks to himself or herself: the desire to gain control. We (or, the characters we portray) try to get control over:

A situation
Another person
Ourselves

The way of gaining control is via thoughts that lead to verbal expression. Tell your students: "Your thoughts are the backbone of any monologue." Make them aware that thoughts

May Lead into verbal expression:
Thought: I can't wait.
Spoken expression: Today we're going to move into our new home. What fun.

May be stronger than the verbal expression:
Thought: Finally, finally, finally I get out of this dump.
Spoken expression: Today we're moving into our new home. What fun.

May be different from the verbal expression:
Thought: Why do we have to move? It's a drag.
Spoken expression: Today we're going to move into our new home. What fun.

Remind your students of the thought process they learned in Part 1 of this book:

Thoughts may be placed before a line:
Thought: What fun.
Spoken expression: Today we're moving into our new home.

Thoughts may be placed after a line:
Spoken expression: Today we're moving into our new home.
Thought: What fun.

Thoughts may be placed in the middle of a line:
Spoken expression: Today we're moving . . .
Thought: What fun.
Spoken expression: into our new home.

Tips *to Help the Very Young Child*

Obviously, the above thought patterns are far too difficult for the very young child. Still, you want to introduce your very young group to the benefits of thoughts. The most effective device, the one directors use in directing young children, is to talk the child through the thought sequence. (On TV and in the movies, the director gives his or her instructions while standing off-camera. Later on, during postproduction, the director's voice will be edited out.)

Before beginning the "thought exercise," have the children select cuddly stuffed toys and soft dolls to hug.

> *Thoughts before a line:*
> Tell your group, "Cuddle your stuffed animal, smile, then say, 'You're the best toy I have. I love you.' "

> *Thoughts after a line:*
> Tell your group, "Now say. 'You're the best toy I have. I love you,' then cuddle your stuffed animal and smile."

> *Thoughts in the middle of a line:*
> Tell your group, "Say. 'You're the best toy I have.' Now cuddle your stuffed animal and smile, then say, 'I love you.' "

Hand out the following practice scene (the monologue) and give your students a little time to memorize it. As the children perform the monologue, *insist* that they interject the spoken words with their thoughts. These thoughts, however, have to be verbalized. You may expect that your group will balk at this (in their words) "babyish and boring" technique. Don't listen to them. Demand that they verbalize their thoughts—only verbalized thoughts are *specific*. Much vague acting goes back to the fact that actors *do not think specific thoughts* in front of the camera but choose thoughts that express their feelings in a haphazard way. Explain to your students that thoughts are the very best controlling device an actor has at his or her disposal. The device of *specifically applied thoughts* leads to

Positive and Negative Reactions
Intensity Levels
Physical Actions

Thoughts that are based upon the actor's own personality and range of experience individualize an actor's performance.

Have your students memorize the following monologue:

Well, it is Mother's birthday and we'll have another family gathering. I used to like those big gatherings when I was a kid.

After your students have memorized this small piece, have them verbalize the thoughts that lead to the appropriate control.

To gain control over a situation:

Well, it's Mother's birthday *(that's a fact I really like)* and we'll have another family gathering *(that's a fact I do not like, but I'll have to live with)*. I used to like those big gatherings when I was a kid *(so I better grin and bear it)*.

To gain control over another person:

Well, it's Mother's birthday *(you better listen to what I have to say)* and we'll have another family gathering *(all right, let me explain)*. I used to like those big gatherings *(now, don't get me wrong)* when I was a kid.

To gain control over yourself:

(All right, calm down) Well, it's Mother's birthday *(I really like that)* and we'll have another family gathering *(calm down, it won't be as bad as it was last year)*. I used to like those big gatherings *(really, I did)* when I was a kid *(and that's the truth)*.

SESSION 3

Physical Actions (I)

Actors ought to know how to perform physical actions in a believable way. Unfortunately, some actors do not *execute* the physical actions a scene demands. They may act (ironing, packing a suitcase, or setting a table) in a general and therefore "acty" way, or they may choose physical actions unrelated to the reality of the scene. For instance: Angie and Burt talk about their vacation plans. Nothing out of the ordinary is supposed to happen in this scene. If, during the conversation, Angie gets up to pour herself a glass of milk, the scene is believable. However, if she aimlessly wanders about, she gives the impression of avoiding Burt, and as such destroys the *reality of the scene.* Make it clear to your students that all physical actions:

Must fit the occasion.
Must be done in a specific way that is right for the scene.

The following are improvisations requiring physical actions:

Look for a lost ring.
    Look underneath the furniture.
    Search your purse.
    Search the couch; remove the pillows and cushions.
    Move books out of a bookcase.

Wrap a present.
    Cut the paper.
    Fold the paper around the present.
    Use tape to secure the edges.
    Choose a ribbon.

Feed your cat.
    Pour milk into a bowl.
    Open a can of cat food (it smells terrible).
    Call your cat.

Fold your laundry.
    Fold pillowcases.
    Fold socks.
    Fold a T-shirt.
    Find a rip in your favorite shirt.

Needless to say, these improvisations require actual props. Hand out the practice scene to be memorized for Session 4.

Tips *to Help the Very Young Child*

All of the above improvisations are suitable for younger children as well.

S E S S I O N 4

Physical Actions (II)

Make certain that the children have memorized their practice scene before you permit them to combine lines with physical actions. Once your students are comfortable performing this combination, ask them to add silent expressions (thoughts), and remind them that thoughts lead to verbal expression and physical actions.

Characters: C (Carol/Chuck)
               D (Dale/Don)

C: I'm telling you, I've had it with school.

D: And I've had it with your empty complaints.

C: I'm not complaining. I mean it. Give me one good reason why I should waste my time in a stuffy schoolroom, listening to a dumb teacher, cramming my brain with useless garbage.

D: You're serious?

C: You bet I am.

D: Listen to me, meathead.

C: Don't be a wise guy.

D: Shut your mouth. Listen to me for once in your life.

C: Okay, okay.

D: So, what do you want to do with your life? Loaf?

C: Of course not. I'm getting a job.

D: What kind of job?

C: Oh . . . I don't know.

D: Think about it. What kind of job? Answer me.

C: Well, I'll find something.

D: No one will hire a dumb kid. Take my advice and stay in school. Buckle down. Get good grades. Graduate. Then think about a job.

Ask your students to perform the practice scene while setting a table and while ironing and folding laundry.
Remind your students:

Pay equal attention to	Thoughts
	Lines
	Physical Actions

Do not "playact" physical actions; perform them realistically.

Ironing:	Use spray starch. Check iron for temperature. Smooth out the items on your ironing board. Look at the item you are ironing.

Folding laundry:	Look for spots and rips. Fold each item neatly.
Setting a table:	Set a neat table.
Watch your Points of Attention:	Objects Partner (other person)
Use communica-tion:	Intensity levels
Use emotional levels:	Positives and negatives

Use thoughts that will lead to verbal expression.

Tips *to Help the Very Young Child*

Even though the combination of physical action and verbal expression seems too complex for younger children, most of them—if the required tasks are simple enough—will respond remarkably well. Here is a suggested practice scene: "The Birthday Invitation."

Characters: A (Amy/Andy)
B (Babs/Bobby)

Scene: *Both children are playing with blocks while they speak their lines.*
You, the director/teacher, should pay close attention that the children really *build* with blocks, and do not act this activity. Permit your actors moments of silence while they concentrate on their blocks.

A: Tomorrow is my birthday.

B: I know.

A: Will you bring me a gift?

B: Do you have a cake?

A: Yes, Mom baked one.

B: What kind of cake?

A: Chocolate cake.

SESSION 5

The Private Moment

Needless to say, your students have to learn how to move comfortably from one acting moment to the next. They have to be taught that each and every moment (regardless of its dramatic impact) demands proper emphasis. The actor must give each moment its due and should keep himself or herself from *anticipating* what will be happening next. The Private Moment improvisation is the perfect exercise to teach your students the concept of moment-to-moment acting. This time your students won't be given a situation to act out or to improvise on. They have to create their own private moment. Supply your group with such basic props as chairs, tables, and boxes, and ask them to bring whatever props they desire. Warn your students that:

No verbal expression will be permitted.
Each physical action must be executed truthfully.

Each private moment improvisation must have a beginning, middle, and end.
It is possible that some of your students are at a loss for what to do. Here are a few suggestions:

Watch TV
Write a letter
Polish your nails
Assemble a toy

Wait for a friend
Clean out your bookcase or closet

Ask the children to keep the private moment simple and as undramatic as possible, and advise them to

Relax
Not think about acting but about *doing.* Go from moment to moment; for example, if one has chosen the private moment of watching TV, the following physical actions are required:
    Check the TV listings for a suitable show.
    Walk to the sideboard, open the cookie jar, and get a cookie.
    Turn on the TV set.
    Settle yourself comfortably.
    Start munching your cookie.
    Enjoy the show.

Most of the children will do well. For the ones who'll find the private moment boring, you may point out that a series of physical actions (private moments) does constitute an important part of most movies and TV shows, and for this very reason the private moment is an exercise they ought to give their full attention to. If you have sufficient time, it might be a good idea to have each student repeat his or her private moment in front of the camera. Only then will your students be able to tell how natural or tense they were. To make this exercise even more interesting (and demanding) give your students the opportunity to decide on floor marks and camera moves to be employed.

A typical taped private moment may look like this:

Pan with student to table
Hold on student and pull in to medium on student as he/she studies TV listings
Pan with student as student walks to sideboard, opens a cookie jar, takes out a cookie, closes the jar, and puts it back on the shelf
Track with student as student walks back to TV set
Hold on student and pull in, as student settles himself/herself in front of set
Pull in to tight medium as student enjoys the show

Your next improvisation—Mob Scene: The Flying Saucer—combines the private moments of a number of characters. A group of people watch a flying saucer land on a school's parking lot. Each and every person reacts in his or her own way. This is the cast:

TV reporter/TV cameraperson
Two children on their way to school
An anxious lady who does not want to watch the flying saucer
A science fiction writer who enjoys the flying saucer
A mother with an unruly child
A father with a bored child
A teacher who wishes her homeroom could watch the event
A police officer who tries to disperse the crowd
An actor who is convinced the flying saucer is nothing but a movie stunt, and looks for the camera crew
A news reporter who comes late to the event

Ask the children to express themselves in verbal and physical actions. This exercise works in two segments:

Segment 1: The children deal with their own reality of the moment.
   Where were they before the incident?
   How do they feel about the incident?
   Are they frightened, elated, curious, disinterested?
Segment 2: The children have to relate to other members in the group.
   What are the characters' physical and emotional condition *after* the initial sighting of the flying saucer?

Tips *to Help the Very Young Child*

The Private Moment exercise, in a simplified form, is ideal for the very young child. Do not interrupt the children as they enjoy their private moments, but give simple suggestions, such as:

Play with your doll, feed your doll, show your doll a picture book, put your doll to bed.

Play with a truck, fill your truck with blocks, take your truck to the gas station to get gas.

String some beads.

Put a puzzle together.

Once your students are comfortable with the exercise, let them repeat their private moment in front of the camera and permit them to participate in the Flying Saucer improvisation.

S E S S I O N   6

Obstacles (the Reality of the Moment)

"Obstacles," you will make clear to your students, "keep you from whatever you want to achieve. In other words, obstacles make it harder, or at times impossible, to achieve your desired goal." Give the children the opportunity to discuss times when they encountered obstacles, and permit them to tell how they dealt with them.

You may mention that while obstacles are a pain in the neck as far as real-life situations are concerned, they are heaven-sent gifts for the actor. A well-defined obstacle, that is to say, an obstacle that gives the actors the opportunity to deal with it in an interesting manner, makes any scene come alive. After you have shown a movie—preferably a comedy—that points out your contention, list the obstacles:

Time-Object Obstacles
Circumstantial Obstacles
Obstacles within Yourself

Time-Object Obstacles: In this improvisation your students will handle real objects (props). Observe your students closely to make certain they deal with the objects in a real and believable way. Do not permit any "acting."

"You are late to school and cannot find your book report that, unfortunately, is due today." The tasks to be accomplished are as follows:

Points of Attention: The watch you wear; the places you look for the book report: your school bag, the desk drawer, among your books, underneath the papers on the desk.

Intensity Levels: Increasing tension as you cannot find the report.

Full-body Relaxation: As you finally find the report.

"You are getting ready for a party." Again your students will handle real props; the girls have to deal with a party dress, the boys with a shirt.

You take out your dress/shirt. Admire it. It is your favorite garment, and you look forward to wearing it.
Then you discover a missing button.
Go to your dresser drawer; search for a button (it takes a little time to find a matching one).
From downstairs your mother calls, "Hurry up, we're ready to leave." Quickly you search for a needle and thread. As you snip off some thread the button drops to the floor.
Frantically you look for the button. You find it the moment you hear your mother's voice: "What are you doing? Hurry up."
You call, "I'll be right down." Hands shaking, you try to thread the needle.
Your mother's voice: "Get down this minute, or we'll leave without you," makes you decide whether you will:
Disregard her voice and sew on the button.
Quickly reach for another dress/shirt.
Leave with the button missing.

Circumstantial Obstacles: This exercise, as with the previous ones, requires real props (pots, pans, boxes to serve as cupboard and refrigerator, a carton of eggs, flowers, tablecloth, silverware, and dishes). Two partners will be assigned to this improvisation: "It is your parents' anniversary. You have decided to surprise them with a delicious breakfast and a beautifully set table. The two of you got up early—your parents are still asleep—and sneaked into the kitchen. You are ready to prepare the most delicious breakfast anyone can imagine."

This improvisation is based on the premise that the two partners achieve their goal without waking their parents, even though everything works against them.

Quietly you try to set a table, but the dishes clatter and a cup drops on the floor and breaks.

You cannot find the eggs. Finally, you discover a dozen way in the back of the refrigerator. As you reach for the carton your robe gets caught in the refrigerator door.

Your partner, busily arranging flowers, gets stung by a bee.

Obstacles within Yourself: The two following improvisations are based on thoughts and Points of Attention *only.*

You want to read a fascinating book, but you have homework to do.

Props: Romance or adventure story, books, pencil, notebook, paper.

You are deciding between two outfits: One is exactly what you have been looking for, but it is expensive. The other outfit is affordable but unexciting.

You know you ought to choose outfit number two, but you are tempted to buy number one.

Leave the decision up to the individual student.

The next improvisation consists of a dialogue between two cousins. It does not require any props.

Cousin L is known as the family braggart. You have been warned to be "nice and hospitable to poor L," and have been instructed to listen politely to her/his tall tales.

This is an improvisation in which your thoughts are the opposite of your spoken words.

The intensity level of your thoughts increases as the desire to tell L off becomes stronger.

Characters: You
　　　　　　　Cousin L

Discuss with your group the fact that each actor should commit himself or herself fully to the given obstacle, regardless of how insignificant the obstacle seems. As the actor deals with the obstacle within himself/herself, he/she should be aware that physical actions are the means to show the audience the character's state of mind. In the "cousin L" exercise the physical actions that keep the character from telling cousin L off may be:

Walking around the room
Drinking a glass of water

SESSION 7

Sense Awareness

This segment's topic is *sense awareness*. Sense awareness requires that actors incorporate the character's awareness of

Environment (pleasant, unpleasant)
Clothing (comfortable, uncomfortable; new, old; attractive, unattractive)
Tasks characters have to perform
Where character has been *before* the beginning of the scene
Where character will be going *after* the scene has ended

Remind your students that sense awareness fine-tunes their performance and is the *final step* to be taken as one works on a scene. Sense awareness explores a character's

Emotional state
Physical state

Most important, sense awareness has to be made visible to the audience by the use of externals; that is, by employing physical actions. Explain to your group that it is not as much your acting responsibility to *feel* happy or tired or inquisitive as to *show* (in a moving way) that you *are* happy, tired, or inquisitive.

"It is a hot day. You are coming home from your PE class. You are sweaty, and your clothes stick to your body. You are thirsty; you pour yourself a glass of water and enjoy it. Dab your face and arms with water. Feel a little more relaxed."

Or: "It is a cold day, and you are coming home from skating. You are chilled to the bone and enjoy the warm refuge of your home. You remove your outer clothing. Take off your boots, rub your toes, wriggle your toes. Then fix yourself a cup of hot chocolate. Savor the drink's sweet fragrance before you enjoy the hot drink, sip by sip."

Mention to your students that both simple exercises demand the believable execution of externals. None of the study should be permitted to blur one *external* into the next. Each of the externals shows a clearly defined beginning, middle, and end.

Once your students are comfortable with the sense awareness of the two above improvisations, add a *verbal* element: "You discover that your sister/brother had 'borrowed' and ruined your best T-shirt—the one that your aunt Agnes had sent all the way from Hawaii. You make it clear that this was the first and last time your brother/sister could ever borrow something of yours."

Make it clear to your group that while the scene *seems* to be about the argument between two siblings, they should pay close attention to sense awareness:

Environment (heat, cold)
Clothing
Where they were before the beginning of the scene

Tips *to Help the Very Young Child*

Again, while the concept of sense awareness is too difficult for the younger children to comprehend, they will do just fine performing the two simple improvisations previously described:

Coming home from PE class
You feel hot and thirsty.
Get yourself a glass of cold water.
Drink the water.
You feel relaxed.

Coming home from skating (or a walk)
Your hands and feet are cold.
You enjoy your nice, warm kitchen.
Ask your mother for a cup of hot chocolate.
Enjoy the chocolate.

Make certain that your students deal fully with the elements of heat and cold stressed in these improvisations.

S E S S I O N 8

Preoccupation

Preoccupation is the next external your students need to know about. First, make sure the children are familiar with the term *preoccupation*; let them discuss times when they were preoccupied. If the discussion lacks vitality, you may help out with these suggestions:

Did you ever think about your vacation, or going shopping, or winning a tennis match while listening to a boring lecture in school?

Did you ever wish you were some other place while you went shopping with your parents?

Were you ever on a baby-sitting job and—while playing a game with your charges—dreamed about this neat new boy/girl in school?

Did you ever try to concentrate on your homework while watching a fascinating program on TV?

After your students understand the concept of preoccupation, explain that while preoccupation does occur in the character's mind, successfully making a character's preoccupation clear to the audience depends on the actor's ability to express it in externals—that is, in physical actions. Explain that a character's preoccupation rarely will be found in the text the actor has at his or her disposal; the actor has to search for it.

Do your best to make certain that your students have grasped the concept of preoccupation and are ready to put it into practice. At this point, question your group as to how they would express preoccupation in physical actions. As an example you may use the following:

You are doing your homework but are daydreaming (*preoccupation*) about your forthcoming school dance, you
> Drum your fingers on the table
> Doodle
> Get up and walk around
> Look through your closet searching for appropriate things to wear
> Every so often go (reluctantly) back to your schoolwork

After this exercise, your students should be given the opportunity to work with real props for the following improvisations:

Task: set a table
Preoccupation: Your mother has invited some friends for lunch. She asks you to set an attractive table. The dishes are delicate and expensive and you are afraid to break them.
External (physical actions)
You carry each dish very carefully to the table.
You touch each cup and saucer gingerly.
You look admiringly at the dishes.
You breathe a sigh of relief after your job has been completed.

Task: set a table
Preoccupation: You are embarrassed because the dishes are chipped and unmatched.
External (physical actions)
Trace some of the dishes with your fingertips to find out whether one or the other is too chipped to be placed on the table.

Replace some of the dishes with others.
Change cups, plates, and saucers around to find the best match.

Task: pack a suitcase
Preoccupation: You are looking forward to the most exciting vacation of your life.
External (physical actions)
Fold garments and place them into a suitcase.
Hold up the garments and dance around.
Pull out a travel folder and—smiling—look at it.
Hug yourself with joy.

Task: pack a suitcase
Preoccupation: You really do not want to go on this vacation. A visit to Aunt Matilda, a stickler for "deportment and good manners," is not much fun.
External (physical actions)
Look at a garment, think about Aunt Matilda; put this particular garment back and search for a more suitable one.
Uninterested, throw your clothes into the suitcase.
Look at your plane ticket and sigh a deep, unhappy sigh.

Remind your students that even though their attention is on the given preoccupation of the scene, they should not fail to execute the given task (setting a table, packing a suitcase) in a real, not acty, way.

PART FOUR

Becoming a Character: Characterization Techniques

Goals (I)

A movie script catches emotions and actions "in flight" and puts them down on paper so the written word will be *heard* and *seen*. The actors involved in this process of "showing," needless to say, have to "get into" the characters to be portrayed.

Your students have explored and excelled in mastering a number of important acting techniques, but so far they have worked on expressing themselves and their own personality. It is important that an actor know how to project his or her personality; after all, the success of any actor is *based* on personality (this holds true for the adult as well as the child actor). But if you intend to remain in this business for a long time, you cannot keep on mirroring yourself all the time. Sooner or later each and every actor has to deal with the problem of characterization.

One may contend that stars play only themselves. This is true to some extent, but how many stars are there in comparison with the working actor? And how many stars, again in comparison with working actors, have staying power?

Too often, unfortunately, even skilled actors

Don a character's attire but remain themselves.
"Act" the character to be portrayed in a manner alien to the personality presented in the script.
Add some slight behavioral touches that give only a fleeting impression of the character portrayed.

Most likely these actors disregard goals—what a character wants to achieve—and subgoals—what a character does to achieve his or her goals.

So let your students take a good look at goals and subgoals. The popular proverb "One picture is worth a thousand words" may be changed to "An improvisation is better than a long explanation" for our purpose. Let's begin with five appropriate improvisations in which one actor is shopping for a new outfit. Use real or imaginary props.

Characters: The Shopper
The Salesperson (Father, Mother, for improvisations 4 and 5)

The student portraying the shopper has to adjust to the following characterizations:
  1. You are your nice, friendly self.
  2. You are an obnoxious, demanding shopper.
  3. You are a vain shopper.
  4. You are a spoiled child.
  5. You are a tired child.

You may expect that while improvisation 1 worked smoothly, all other improvisations left much to be desired. The Lauras and Mary Anns in your group performed one-dimensionally, and the Timmys took the chance to fall back into their old habit of hamming it up. All are unhappy about the way they performed.

Tell your students that their performances were unsatisfactory because goals, the first step toward effective characterization, were missing. Assure them that goals are not complicated if they keep in mind that a goal is something a character *wants to do or achieve*. Let your students discuss some goals they encounter every day.

Situation: You have planned a day at the beach.

Goals: I want to listen to the weather forecast.
I want to get my beach things together.
I want to buy some sunscreen.

Situation: You have to take an important test.

Goals: I want to get my books and notes organized.
             I want to study hard.
             I want my dad to quiz me.

Before you attempt to venture any further into the thicket called goals, ask your students: "What is the shopper's goal in our improvisation? What does the shopper want to do?"

Invariably you will be rewarded with the answer: "Easy. The shopper wants to buy an outfit."

"Well," you may reply, "you are right and you are wrong." When we speak about goals, we are actually speaking about two kinds: the *open goal* and the *hidden goal*.

In our improvisation the open goal is, wanting to buy an outfit, while the hidden goal expresses *why* a character wants something and therefore behaves in a certain way. Of the two goals, the hidden goal is the more interesting one to perform.

To demonstrate this principle, show the children a brightly wrapped package and say, "This is the open goal—a box, paper, and a pretty ribbon; very attractive, but not too exciting." Open the package, take out a funny stuffed toy, and say, "The hidden goal is what's inside the package. When you receive a present, you are after what's inside the package; when you act you are after the hidden goal." Making certain that your students have some understanding of open goals and hidden goals, continue to discuss the Shopping for an Outfit improvisation in detail.

1. You are your nice, friendly self.
   Open Goal: I want to buy an outfit.
   Hidden Goal: I want to enjoy my shopping trip.

2. You are an obnoxious, demanding shopper.
   Open Goal: I want to buy an outfit.
   Hidden Goal: I want to show the salesperson that I am boss.

3. You are a vain shopper.
   Open Goal: I want to buy an outfit.
   Hidden Goal: I want to admire myself.

4. You are a spoiled child.
   Open Goal: I want to buy an outfit.

Hidden Goal: I want to force my mother/father to buy a certain outfit. If he/she won't, I am determined to make this shopping trip a miserable experience for my parent.

5. You are a tired child.
   Open Goal: I want to buy an outfit.
   Hidden Goal: I am tired and I want to go home.

After you're convinced that your students do understand the concept of hidden goals, begin with the improvisations. It may, however, be a good idea to have them begin each exercise with a few memorized lines before they take off on their own. (Try to supply your group with some outfits for props.)

Characters: Shopper
            Salesperson (Mom, Dad, in improvisations 4 and 5)

1. You are a friendly shopper.
   Hidden Goal: I want to enjoy my shopping trip.

SHOPPER: You have so many great outfits here. I don't know which one to buy.

SALESPERSON: Yes, I know. We offer wonderful merchandise.

SHOPPER: What do you think? Is the T-shirt a better match to my jeans, or is the embroidered shirt?

SALESPERSON: How about buying both? Today we have a 50-percent-off special sale.

SHOPPER: Really? Yes, I'll take both.

2. You are an obnoxious shopper.
   Hidden Goal: I want to show the salesperson that I am the boss.

SHOPPER: I cannot find a thing . . . everything you have shown me is disgusting.

SALESPERSON: Well, we have some painted T-shirts.

SHOPPER: Painted T-shirts. You must be kidding. If I wanted to buy T-shirts I'd go to a flea market or a discount store, not a fancy boutique, like yours is *supposed* to be.

SALESPERSON: May I show you some embroidered shirts?

SHOPPER: Don't bother. I won't find anything suitable here.

3. You are a vain shopper.
   Hidden Goal: I want to admire myself.

SHOPPER: How do you like this T-shirt on me? Don't you think it looks great? I just can't decide, though, whether to get the blue or the green.

SALESPERSON: We have many nice colors in that line of shirts.

SHOPPER: Maybe I should get both the green and the blue one. You know, not many people can wear these colors, but they look good on *me*.

4. You are a spoiled child.
   Hidden Goal: I want to force my mother/father to buy a certain outfit.

SHOPPER: I don't like little teddy bears on my T-shirt. I want the one with the spaceship.

MOM/DAD: No. The teddy bear shirt is on sale. The spaceship shirt is too expensive.

SHOPPER: I want the spaceship.

MOM/DAD: Sorry. No. Either the teddy bears or nothing.

SHOPPER *(Throws himself/herself on the floor):* I want the spaceship.

MOM/DAD: Get up right now, or you won't get anything.

SHOPPER: That's fine with me.

5. You are a tired child.
   Hidden Goal: I want to go home.

MOM/DAD: I promise, this is the last store we are going to.

SHOPPER *(Whines):* I want to go home. I'm tired.

MOM/DAD: We only have to get a few T-shirts for you, and home we go.

SHOPPER: Can't we go home now? Buy the shirts tomorrow. Please?

MOM/DAD: Sorry. I have to go to work tomorrow.

SHOPPER: Okay.

Tips *to Help the Very Young Child*

Goals are a difficult enough topic for the adult actor and should not be discussed with the young child. However, because your little ones at times will work together with your older students, they will be exposed to the term *goal.* I suggest you say: "A goal is something you *want to do,* like":

I want to play with my cat.
I want to eat an ice-cream cone.
I want to go swimming.

Take time to talk with your very young students about things they want and like to do, before you tell them the story about "The Little Engine That Could." "Once upon a time there was a little train. All its cars were loaded with toys for boys and girls. Lots and lots of toys. But there was a steep hill, and as soon as the train got to this hill, the engine stopped. As hard as the engine tried, it could not go on. How sad. Now the children had to forget about all those wonderful toys. But, instead of turning around, the brave little engine said, 'I *think* I can . . . I *think* I can . . . I *think* I can . . . I *think* I can . . . and what do you know, I *can*—I *can*.' The brave little engine pulled the train over the steep hill. So tell me, what did the engine *want to do*?"

"Get the train over the hill."

"Right, you've got it. And why did it want to get the train over the hill?"

"To get the toys to the children."

"Exactly. So the train's goal was to get the train over the hill."

Have the children—hands on each other's shoulders—form a "snake line." Slowly first then faster and faster have them stomp their feet and call out, "I *think* I can . . . I *think* I can . . . I *think* I can . . . I *think* I can . . . I *can*—I *can*—I *can*—I *can*."

Next you introduce improvisations on goal exercises "the happy shopper," "the spoiled child," and "the tired child." Refrain from long explanations, but simply say:

1. Imagine your parent takes you shopping. You have lots and lots of fun looking for a neat outfit.

Before you begin the exercise, have the children tell about the best outfit they could imagine.

4. And now you dislike every outfit in sight, and you enjoy being nasty to the salesperson and your parent.

Again have the children verbalize their impression of an outfit they would not like to wear.

5. You are very tired, and you want to go home. You do not care whether or not your parent buys an outfit for you.

Ask the children about a shopping trip that was tiresome, and let them tell you about it.

Try improvisations first. Only if your very young group encounters difficulties should you give them some help with lines.

1. The happy shopper:
   All the T-shirts are neat. I love the one with the teddy bears. No, the kittens are much cuter. No, no, I want the spaceship—the spaceship is it. Please buy me the spaceship.

4. The spoiled shopper:
   Come on, Mom/Dad, let's go to another store. I don't like anything here. No, no, no. I don't like anything.

5. The tired shopper:
   I want to go home. I'm tired. We've been shopping all day long. I've had enough.

S E S S I O N   2

Goals (II)

Congratulate the children on the good job they did in Session 1 before you continue to explore goals.

In the last session we worked on goals and hidden goals; now we will discover where these goals lead us. First of all, and this is very important, don't confuse goals with emotions. Some actors—even professional ones—worry about how a character feels in a certain situation, and they forget about what the character wants to do or achieve. This is a list of feelings:

happy
sad
nervous
bossy

Always remember: Feelings and emotions cannot be portrayed without an appropriate goal to back them up.

The key to whether you are to portray a feeling or a goal is simple: The words *to be* tell you you are searching for a feeling; the words *I want to* (and an added action verb such as *run, search, comfort*) tell you you are portraying a goal.

"But isn't acting all about emotions and feelings?" one student may ask.

"Yes," you will agree, "acting is about emotion. But the emotions shown on the screen must be caused by something."

"The goal?"

"You've got it. Your character's *emotion* is based on the satisfaction or frustration of your character's *goal*. Let's talk about yesterday's improvisation. Remember the Shopping for an Outfit improvisation?"

You will be rewarded with nods.

"The shopper is happy, right?"

More nods.

"The open goal was 'I want to buy an outfit,' and the hidden goal was 'I want to enjoy my shopping trip.' " Your group agrees.

"Now, if the shopper finds just the right outfit, will his/her goal be satisfied?"

"Yes."

"As a result, what is his/her emotion?"

"The shopper is happy."

"Terrific, but if the shopper cannot find a single thing he/she likes, do you think the shopper will still enjoy the shopping trip—will he/she still be happy?"

"Of course not." Your students have grasped the concept.

"Right. The satisfaction or frustration of a goal causes a character's emotions."

Next suggest to your students that they replace the feelings stated on the *to be* side into goals of *I want to:*

To be kind	I want to help
To be shy	I want to hide
To be lazy	I want to avoid (doing anything)
To be nervous	I want to guard (myself)
To be confident	I want to stress (my dignity)
To be sarcastic	I want to put (another) down
To be bossy	I want to dominate

The following are some situations that will lead to the discussion of goals. Make your group aware that different goals—based on the same situation—lead to different emotions. Work on the following improvisations:

You have been invited to a birthday party.
    I want to get (on the good side of everyone).
    I want to capture (the attention of everyone).
    I want to boss (everyone around).
    I want to brighten (the party).
It is Christmastime and you work out a budget for your Christmas purchases.
    I want to discover (how much I can spend).
    I want to guard (against spending too much).
    I want to work (with my budget. I do not have enough money for all the presents I want to buy).

You are the new kid on the block and the new kid in school.
  I want to meet (the other students).
  I want to gain (the others' confidence).
  I want to show (that I am an interesting person).

Tips to Help the Very Young Child

Start this session by asking, "Do you remember our 'Little Engine That Could' story and our game as we pretended to be the little engine? What did we do?"

  "We stomped our feet, we yelled, and walked faster and faster."

  "Right, that's what we did. So you see, we *did something*." Ask your group what they would do if their goals were:

  I want to show how happy I am.
  I want to fall asleep.
  I want to sneak a cookie out of the kitchen.
  I want to keep myself from crying after I fell and hurt myself.
  I want to force myself to pet the puppy.
  I want to show the kitten how much I love it.

Again, give your students the opportunity to use creativity as they improvise on the given topics. Only if one of the children gets tense or bored will you direct him or her. Here are some suggestions:

  I want to *show* how happy I am:
    Hand your student a prettily wrapped package; let him/her eagerly unwrap it and take out a toy, clap hands, and jump for joy.

  I want to *fall* asleep:
    Ask your student to grab a few pillows, lie down, take hold of a stuffed animal, cuddle the toy, stretch, yawn, close his/her eyes, and sleep.

  I want to *sneak* a cookie out of the kitchen:
    Tiptoe to the corner of the room. Look around to make certain that no one sees you. Then carefully, ever so carefully, lift the lid off the

cookie jar, take out a cookie, and munch it. Looking as innocently as you can manage, walk out of the room.

I want to *keep* from crying after I fell and hurt myself:
Imagine you scraped your knee. With a washcloth you wash off the dirt. Force yourself to look at your knee to find out whether you are bleeding. Grit your teeth to keep yourself from crying.

I want to *force* myself to pet the puppy:
(Put the stuffed dog a few steps away from the child working on the improvisation.) Walk closer to the puppy, slowly and carefully. Look at the puppy before you reach out to pat it a little.

I want to *show* the kitten how much I love it:
(Supply your student with a stuffed cat.) Pick up the kitten; feel how soft it is. It is still very small and fragile. Handle it carefully. Do not squeeze it when you hug it. Smile and enjoy looking at the kitten.

S E S S I O N   3

The Important If

This session is devoted to the important *if*. The important *if* refers to the goal the actor would choose if he or she were the *character*. Remind the students that a goal is something the character wants to do or achieve and explain that a goal should not be chosen because you think it is effective and may look great on stage or screen but because it is the goal *you* would choose.

Discuss with your students the important *if* that each one of them would choose for the following situations:

You are alone at home and hear someone entering the house.

You have received a birthday package from your favorite aunt and you are tempted to open it, but know you should wait until your mother is home.

You are grocery shopping. At the checkout counter you discover you have left your money at home.

The following scene gives your students the opportunity to practice the important *if*:

Characters: E (Ed/Emelie)
              F (Fred/Fran)
Situation: E is on the phone with his/her friend, when F wants to use the phone.
E—*Open Goal:* I want to keep possession of the phone.
E—*Hidden Goal:* I want to stop being a doormat.

F—*Open Goal:* I want the phone for myself.
F—*Hidden Goal:* I want to establish my superiority.

Remind your students that these are only *suggested* goals, and they ought to use the important *if* to arrive at goals of their own.

E *(On the phone):* Is that true? No, you must be kidding. Don't tell me. What did he say?

F saunters by. Seeing that E is on the phone, he or she points to the phone.

E *(Looks at F):* Can't you see I'm on the phone?

F: That phone is not your personal property. I want to make a call.

E *(Into phone):* I can't believe it. That's fantastic.

F: I have to make a call.

E *(Turns to F):* Stop bothering me. *(Into phone)* No, of course I don't mean you; my pesky brother(sister) is bothering me.

F: Are you going to stay on the phone all night? Come on, let me have it.

E: Just one sec. Listen . . . I'll be through in a moment. *(Into phone)* Really, I have to know everything about that. . . . *(To F)* I'll be through in a sec I told you.

F: That's what you always say. Give me the phone.

Tips *to Help the Very Young Child*

Even young children—especially in kindergarten plays—will encounter fictional situations alien to them—and as a result, have to portray unfamiliar emotions. The older child has the important *if* to fall back on. But what about younger children? Should the director or teacher skip this important and helpful technique since little kids may not understand it? Should the director or teacher demand of the young child to show an emotion the child neither understands nor is able to feel?

To illustrate my point, let's use the scene when Little Red Riding Hood meets the wolf, disguised as Grandmother. If the child knows that the wolf is actor Jim, then she portrays a fear she doesn't feel; she learns poor acting habits, leading to phony acting.

If, however, she is told that this scary creature, the wolf, may hurt her, the door to future emotional problems has been opened.

So what to do? From early on, all children use make-believe when they play with their toys. Since make-believe is very natural and comfortable for the small child, begin "directing" the child by saying, "We are going to tell a story, and we make it lots of fun by having you make believe that you, Jane, are Little Red Riding Hood, Jim is the wolf, Kathy is the grandmother, and Chuck is the hunter. And we *act* out the story."

Show Jane, Little Red Riding Hood, the mask that Jim the wolf wears. Let her handle it, even let her try it on herself, and look at herself in the mirror.

But, you may ask, how do I get her to portray fear? This is the moment when the important *if* comes in handy for *you* the director or teacher, as you translate Little Red Riding Hood's fear into unthreatening physical actions that show fear.

"Imagine," you may say, "that you carry eggs in your basket, and since you know how easily eggs break, you walk very carefully, very slowly toward your grandmother's bed. There you look at the wolf—take your time; take a good long look before you reach out to touch the wolf's face. Remember when your mom bakes cookies? And remember how after the cookies are out of the oven you touch one of them very, very carefully because you don't want to burn your finger? This is exactly how you touch the wolf's face. Next, as the wolf grabs your basket and jumps out of bed, you'll run to the door. Remember the races you have in kindergarten? Remember the time when you won the race? Well, that's the way you run to the door."

After you have prepared the children, you'll introduce your group to the practice scene "In Grandmother's Cottage."

Characters: Little Red Riding Hood
                 Wolf

Little Red Riding Hood knocks at the door.

WOLF: Who is it?

LITTLE RED RIDING HOOD: It's me, Grandmother. Your Little Red Riding Hood.

Wolf smiles a nasty smile.

WOLF *(Whispers):* Finally I get the basket of goodies. . . .

Wolf slips under the covers.

WOLF: Come on in . . .

The wolf's voice does not sound soft and sweet. The wolf jumps out of bed, races to the washstand, gets some mouthwash, gurgles, swallows, and jumps back into bed.

WOLF *(Falsetto):* . . . my sweet little granddaughter.

Little Red Riding Hood enters.

WOLF: How sweet of you to visit your old, sick grandmother.

LITTLE RED RIDING HOOD: I brought you some cake and cookies.

WOLF *(His voice falsetto again):* Let's have the grub . . . Oh, I'm much too sick to eat cake, but let me see it anyway.

Hesitantly Little Red Riding Hood walks to the bed, but all of a sudden she stops.

WOLF: What's the matter?

LITTLE RED RIDING HOOD: Your voice. Grandmother, your voice is so . . .

WOLF: Raspy? I have a cold (*coughs*)—a very, very bad cold.

Little Red Riding Hood walks closer.

WOLF: Hurry up, I don't have all day.

By now Little Red Riding Hood is standing close to the bed. The wolf reaches for the basket, but Little Red Riding Hood holds on to it. As the wolf moves toward her, she touches his face.

LITTLE RED RIDING HOOD: Grandmother, your eyes are so big.

WOLF: So I can see you better.

LITTLE RED RIDING HOOD: Grandmother, your mouth is so big.

WOLF: So I can eat—

Wolf jumps out of bed, tries to grab the basket, but Little Red Riding Hood is faster. She runs to the door.

WOLF: —the cake in one big bite.

The door slams behind Little Red Riding Hood. Sadly the wolf collapses on the bed. He reaches for a glass of water and a cracker.

WOLF: Let's have a spot of tea anyway.

At the end of this session, hand out the practice scene "Poor Cinderella." Ask your students to memorize parts appropriate for their ages. If you are combining the young children with the older ones, the young ones can be given the parts of the mice.

Characters: Cinderella
Stepmother
Stepsister Annabelle
Stepsister Miranda
Lucifer, the cat

The mice (your very young children)
Rascal Mouse
Pretty Mouse
Shy Mouse
Nosy Mouse

Beat 1

Scene: *Cinderella's kitchen, late afternoon. Lucifer the cat snores in front of the fireplace. The mice, hiding under the table and under chairs, eye him fearfully. Cinderella, sitting next to Lucifer on the floor, sews a lace collar on a silk dress. We hear Annabelle's shrill voice.*

ANNABELLE: Cinderella! Cinderella! Cinderella!

Annabelle enters.

ANNABELLE: Stop fooling around with my dress.

CINDERELLA: Almost ready.

ANNABELLE: What's keeping you? Hurry up.

CINDERELLA: I have to sew slowly and carefully. I want to sew a fine seam. This dress has to look perfect. You are going to wear it to Prince Charming's ball. (*For a moment she permits herself to dream about the ball and sighs*) Prince Charming.

Lucifer awakens, stretches, brushes his whiskers.

LUCIFER: Meow. Cinderella, you lazy girl, do your work. Don't talk so much.

CINDERELLA: Be quiet. Oh, this lace is so difficult to sew.

Cinderella, intent on her work, pricks her finger.

CINDERELLA: Ouch!

ANNABELLE: You stupid girl.

She tears the dress away from Cinderella.

LUCIFER: Stupid girl. Meow. Meow.

Miranda rushes in.

MIRANDA: What's happening?

LUCIFER *(Sidles up to Miranda):* Look what she did. There's a big drop of nasty blood on Annabelle's pretty dress.

ANNABELLE *(To Cinderella):* You clumsy girl.

CINDERELLA: I am so sorry, Annabelle. I'll wash it off.

ANNABELLE: And spot the silk? You're not only clumsy . . .

LUCIFER *(Grins):* Really klutzy . . .

ANNABELLE: You're stupid. Do you hear me? *(Her voice rises)* Stupid.

While Annabelle and Lucifer insult Cinderella, Miranda tries to push through to her. Finally she succeeds. Her hair is in curlers.

MIRANDA: My hair is dry. Hurry, Cinderella, take the curlers off.

ANNABELLE: First she has to clean my dress and sew the lace on *(she pushes Miranda to the side).*

MIRANDA: No, she has to do my hair *(pushes Annabelle to the side).*

ANNABELLE: My dress *(pushes Miranda).*

MIRANDA: My hair *(grabs Annabelle).*

Cinderella, courageously, tries to get the sisters apart. She fails.
While the two sisters are fighting, Lucifer has detected Pretty Mouse. Meowing, he chases her. Shy Mouse, Nosy Mouse, and Rascal Mouse hide. They try to show Pretty Mouse where to hide. But Pretty Mouse, distracted by a mirror, admires herself. Lucifer has almost caught her, when Rascal Mouse pulls Pretty Mouse to safety.
Stepmother, carrying a dress, storms into the room.

Beat 2

STEPMOTHER: Quit arguing, girls. Act like ladies—like the sweet girls you are.

Lucifer, behind the stepmother's back, makes a face indicting that the girls are not sweet.

STEPMOTHER: Remember, Prince Charming will choose one of you for his bride.

Lucifer, behind the stepmother's back, indicates that the Prince will never choose one of the sisters, but the moment the stepmother turns he nods, smiles sweetly, and throws kisses to Miranda and Annabelle.

ANNABELLE: He'll choose me.

MIRANDA: No, me.

ANNABELLE: Me.

They grab each other, ready to fight. Skillfully, the stepmother pulls them apart. Lucifer dances around the stepmother.

LUCIFER: There are mice in this room . . . many, many greedy, cheese-eating mice.

STEPMOTHER: Don't bother me, Lucifer.

LUCIFER: I'll catch them. Meow. I'll catch each and every one of them. Meow.

The mice, listening to his threat, shake. They huddle together.

LUCIFER: I'm a good cat, a good mouser.

Lucifer pounds his chest. But the stepmother pushes Lucifer aside.

STEPMOTHER: I said don't bother me.

The mice are relieved. Nosy Mouse moves a little out of his/her hiding place to get a better look at what is going on.

ANNABELLE: Cinderella ruined my dress.

MIRANDA: Cinderella has to do my hair.

STEPMOTHER: Quiet, you two. Cinderella has to iron *my* dress.

She hands Cinderella a dress.

STEPMOTHER: And be careful you don't scorch it.

LUCIFER *(Whispers):* She hasn't paid for it yet . . .

STEPMOTHER: Don't ruin it.

LUCIFER: 'Cause she's going to take it back to the store after the ball.

CINDERELLA: I will do my very best, Stepmother, dear.

Cinderella reaches for the iron, but the cord has been tangled up. She tries to untangle the cord, as Annabelle and Miranda converge on her again.

MIRANDA: Do my hair first.

ANNABELLE: No, my dress.

RASCAL MOUSE: Let's help Cinderella.

The mice come out of hiding; they help Cinderella untangle the cord. Lucifer sneaks up to the mice on silent paws, but Rascal Mouse discovers the cat.

RASCAL MOUSE: Watch out!

Quickly the mice go back into hiding, and Cinderella, watched by Stepmother, Miranda, and Annabelle, begins ironing. But she enjoys only a few moments of peace. Annabelle puts her dress on the ironing board, and Miranda demands to have her curlers taken off.
Cinderella has no other choice but to iron Stepmother's dress, take out Miranda's curlers, clean Annabelle's dress, faster and faster, until she whirls around like a spinning top.
Lucifer, enjoying her distress, mimicking an orchestra leader, conducts a nonexisting orchestra.

Beat 3

CINDERELLA: Stepmother, dear.

STEPMOTHER: Keep on working; you've finally got your rhythm going.

Lucifer nods; he conducts his nonexisting orchestra faster now.

CINDERELLA: Stepmother, dear, may I ask you a question?

Cinderella takes a deep breath before she blurts it out.

CINDERELLA: I want to go to Prince Charming's ball.

Stepmother, Annabelle, and Miranda stand frozen; Lucifer stops conducting; all stare at Cinderella. The mice come out of their hiding places. There is a moment of shocked silence.

NOSY MOUSE: Cinderella received an invitation.

PRETTY MOUSE: All she needs is a pretty dress.

SHY MOUSE: She'll look beautiful.

STEPMOTHER: What a preposterous idea.

MIRANDA: You have nothing to wear.

ANNABELLE: You're not pretty enough.

LUCIFER: You don't know how to dance.

Lucifer demonstrates a few dance steps.
Stepmother takes her dress, and so does Annabelle. Led by Miranda and followed by Lucifer, they prance out of the room.
Cinderella calls after them.

CINDERELLA: I thought maybe you might lend me a dress, Annabelle. You have so many, Miranda. How about a real old one?

Beat 4

But no one answers. After having made certain that Lucifer is out of the way, the mice gather around Cinderella.

RASCAL MOUSE: You will go to the ball.

PRETTY MOUSE: You'll get your dress.

NOSY MOUSE: All we have to do is . . .

SHY MOUSE: Call your Fairy Godmother.

The mice start calling.

MICE *(Simultaneously):* Fairy Godmother. Fairy Godmother!

CINDERELLA: Fairy Godmother.

Tips *to Help the Very Young Child*

Give your little ones the chance to perform with the older kids; they'll love it. The parts of the mice are perfect for your very young group.

SESSION 4

Practice Performance

One or two sessions might be devoted to the performance of the preceding practice scene. The main emphasis should be placed on the various characters' goals. Make certain to explain to your group that even though the fairy-tale characters are overdrawn, you want to bestow a certain reality upon them by searching for goals that are based on what you would do *if* you were this certain character in this specific situation.

Cinderella

Open Goal: I want to go to the ball.
Hidden Goal: I want to make my dreams come true.
Do not play a clichéd, sweet Cinderella. Base the characterization on
    Cinderella's open and hidden goals. The same holds true for all
    the other characters, as in the following examples.

Lucifer

Open Goal: I want to make life miserable for Cinderella.
Hidden Goal: I want to enjoy my unique position of being the beloved
    cat.
Do not play a nasty Lucifer.

Stepmother

Open Goal: I want to put everything in order.
Hidden Goal: I want to wield power over everyone.
Do not play a mean stepmother.

Annabelle

Open Goal: I want to have things my way.
Hidden Goal: I want to establish my superiority over Miranda.
Do not play an angry Annabelle.

Miranda

Open Goal: I want things my way.
Hidden Goal: I want to hurt Cinderella because she is prettier than I
    am.
Do not play a conceited Miranda.

SESSION 5

Subgoals and Beats

Start this session with the remark "The goals you have worked on so diligently during the past sessions—open goals and hidden goals—refer to what

is called the *main goal*, which pertains to what a character *wants to achieve*. In a movie or TV show each character's main goal must be compelling enough to last throughout the entire script."

The Wizard of Oz	Dorothy	I want to go back to Kansas.
Peter Pan	Peter	I want to remain a child forever.
Snow White and the Seven Dwarfs	Snow White	I want to save myself from the wicked queen.

You will notice that all of the above-given main goals are open goals, but the hidden goal might be even more fun to portray.

The Wizard of Oz	Dorothy	I want to feel secure again.
Peter Pan	Peter	I want to disregard responsibility.
Snow White and the Seven Dwarfs	Snow White	I want others to protect me.

After you have made certain your students are familiar with all aspects of goals, move on to subgoals. Make it clear that, besides main goals, each script offers the opportunity for a series of subgoals.

"Each subgoal," you explain, "*must* lead the character you portray closer to the main goal."

Undoubtedly one of your Timmys will pipe up: "But how do we know where a subgoal is?"

"That's a good question, and I'm glad you asked it"—you praise your bright student—"and there is a simple answer to it: A subgoal starts whenever a situation changes. This means—and this is important—the moment a situation changes, subgoals change for everyone in the scene."

This change is called a *beat*.

Go back to the practice scene on pages 107–113, and discuss the various beats with your group.

Beat 1:   Cinderella works on the dress; stepsisters demand her attention.

Beat 2:   Stepmother comes upon the scene and demands all attention for herself.

Beat 3:   Cinderella asks permission to go to the ball.

Beat 4:   The mice try to help Cinderella.

A subgoal spans either a short or an extended period of time. Since a subgoal helps to move a situation ahead, it *must be specific*, never vague. For instance:

Cinderella works on Annabelle's dress:

> I want to do a good job   (too vague)
>
> I want to sew on the lace as neatly as possible   (specific)

Equally important is the fact that each subgoal must have a *cap*—the moment when the subgoal has been either satisfied or frustrated.

Going back to the practice scene on pages 107–113, take time to discuss the various characters' subgoals for each beat:

Beat 1

Cinderella	I want to satisfy everyone's demand.
Lucifer	I want to make Cinderella look bad.
Annabelle	I want to let my anger out on pretty Cinderella. I will be a wallflower.
Miranda	I want to take the limelight away from Annabelle.

Beat 2

Cinderella	I want to keep myself away from the raging argument.
Stepmother	I want to bring order into this chaos.
Lucifer	I want to get on Stepmother's good side.
Annabelle	I want to get my mother's attention.
Miranda	I want to get my mother's attention away from Annabelle.

Beat 3

Cinderella	I want to force myself to ask permission to go to the ball.
Stepmother	I want to disregard Cinderella's preposterous request.
Lucifer	I want to put Cinderella down.

Beat 4

| Mice | We want to encourage Cinderella to go to the ball. |

Most important:

Each character's subgoal *must* arise from the actor's awareness of what is happening with the characters surrounding him or her. For instance: Cinderella's subgoal—"I want to force myself to ask permission to go to the ball"—becomes more and more difficult to achieve as Cinderella has to face the sneering cat and her overbearing stepmother.

But a word of warning: The acting tool of subgoals is not for everyone in your group. Even for adult acting students, subgoals are not easy to grasp. Some in your group will take to subgoals easily; others will vent their frustration. Therefore, at the first indication of frustration, drop the subject of subgoals.

Tips *to Help the Very Young Child*

In this session give very young children the opportunity to adjust to each other and the characters in the scene.

Beat 1	The mice *hide* from Lucifer, the cat.
Beats 2–3	The mice *pay attention* to what happens. Forgetting about the cat, they come to Cinderella's assistance.
Beat 4	The mice, *supporting* Cinderella, gather around her.

It is fun to work on the mice's characterizations, by giving each of them specific *human* characteristics.

Rascal Mouse	Likes to mimic Tarzan's behavior by standing up very straight while pounding his/her chest.
Pretty Mouse	Always looks into a mirror; admiringly touches his/her hair and outfit.
Shy Mouse	Giggles nervously and keeps his/her eyes downcast.
Nosy Mouse	Always has to be out front. Pushes other mice aside. Has quick head movements. Rubs his/her hands with glee.

S E S S I O N 6

Animal Exercises (I)

Animal exercises are of great help in detailing a character's physical characterization of

Posture
Walking
Body, head, and hand movements

Close attention to these areas will fine-tune any performance. Unfortunately, many actors—a number of skilled, professional actors among them—either disregard the above areas of physical characterization or deal with them in a stilted way. They "perform" physical characteristics, but they don't make them come alive.

Begin this session by showing your students an appropriate film or TV show. No cartoons, please, but real nature shows that show various animals in their natural habitats. After the viewing ask your students to explain and show:

How did the animal run?
How did the animal walk?

How did the animal stalk (if appropriate)?
How does the animal eat?
How does the animal use its paws?
What does the animal use to attack? (Mouth? Claws?)
How does the animal groom itself?
In what way does the animal look at other animals?
How does the animal sleep?

Show a nature film about mice and cats before you ask your students to work on the following improvisations in groups:

Mice are looking for food. One of them discovers a tempting slice of cheese in a strange contraption (a trap). The mice are inspecting the cheese, when a cat approaches. The mice scamper to safety.
Several cats are curled up asleep on the floor. One awakes, stretches, then grooms itself before it walks to the cat bowl and begins lapping milk. Soon the other cats wake up, and as they try to push the first cat away from the bowl, a fight ensues.

And now, paying primary attention to Lucifer the cat and the mice, the children will repeat the practice scene on pages 107–113.
The next logical step is to incorporate animal qualities into the portrayal of characters. Here are some suggestions:

Stepmother   Snake
Stepsisters   Cackling Geese
Cinderella   Hardworking Spider

Stepmother   Buzzard
Stepsisters   Peacocks
Cinderella   Brown Sparrow searching for crumbs

Tips *to Help the Very Young Child*

All of the listed animal exercises are suitable for your very young group.

S E S S I O N   7

Animal Exercises (II)

This session leads your students closer to an animal's inner life of courage, fear, satisfaction, and greed. Practice with your group:

The intense gaze of a lion
The regal gait of a leopard
The relaxed, stretched-out sleeping position of a cat
The determined crawl of a spider
The waddle of a goose hurrying to the pond

Once the children are comfortable doing these animal movements, ask them to add (possible) animal thoughts:

The captive lion: How boring all these creatures are. Why do they stare at me? I don't like them, I want them to leave. I'd better roar my best lion roar to get rid of them. Good, some of them are leaving. I wonder when someone will come to bring my food.

Bear in the forest: I like the way my muscles move. I like the way the sun feels so warm on my fur. I'm hungry. Maybe I should go over to where those creatures—the ranger calls them tourists—are; they always have some goodies.

Cat on a windowsill: I have it made. Life couldn't be any better. I am the beloved pet. Tommy the cat. Whatever I want I get. I only have to slink up to my lady, and she will open a can of delicious-smelling food. Ah, I hear the can opener, so I better jump off the windowsill and hurry into the kitchen.

Mouse: Run, run . . . dear me, where is my hiding place . . . run, run . . . no, not this way . . . there is that cat after me again . . . run . . . run. . . .

Spider: Just a few more push-ups, a pull here, a tuck there, and I'll have it made. It is not easy to spin a web as strong and sturdy as mine are. Not every spider is as skilled as I am.

Duck: Come on, girls, let's get to the pond. The water is muddy. Just right to eat all kinds of good stuff. Come on, girls, what are you waiting for? Once in the water we'll look as graceful as those conceited swans over there.

Ask the children to verbalize their thoughts as they do the animals' movements.

You may expect that one of your Timmys will point out that spiders are *not* animals. Agreeing with him for the sake of simplicity, point out that to make the topic easier, spiders will be considered in the animal exercises.

Tips *to Help the Very Young Child*

Practice the above exercises with the younger children, but you do the verbalization for them.

SESSION 8

The Magic If

A few sessions ago we worked on the important *if*. Today the magic *if* will be the topic.

The magic *if*, as with the animal exercises, helps the actor to work on specific characterization details in the areas of gait, posture, and movements.

Ask your children how many times someone directing a school play has asked them to walk like a prince or princess. This advice, unfortunately, results in a stilted gait and gives rise to unnatural acting. We all have seen royalty on TV. Do they walk any differently from you and me? Of course not. So, why not employ the magic *if*, to overcome any possible walking and posture problems?

Here are a few examples:

Walk like royalty. Walk as if you are balancing a basket filled with apples on your head.

You are afraid to open a door. Touch the door gingerly, as if any quick motion may activate an explosive device.

You are uncertain about a situation you'll have to face. Walk as if you are walking among eggs and are afraid you may break one, or walk as if you are approaching a vicious dog.

Give your students the opportunity to create a few *as if* situations of their own.

As uncomplicated as the magic *if* seems (and children will have fun performing *as if* improvisations), it is imperative that your students learn to give specific details to a character's specific physical actions for a given specific situation. Ask your students "to go all out" as they create these specific details. Here is an example:

You are getting ready for a test.

You are an ambitious student. You are well prepared to take the test.
　　Enter the room with firm steps, your head held high, as if you were listening to a band playing a lively tune.
　　　　Sit down, open your school bag, and take out pencils and notebook as if you were setting up a chessboard.
You are lazy; you have not prepared for the test. You don't care whether you pass or fail.
　　You enter the room chewing bubble gum. Your arms and legs are as uncoordinated as if you were a rag doll.
　　　　You plop onto your seat as if you were an apple dropping to the ground.
　　　　Finally you hunt in your school bag for your supplies. You are as hesitant as if the bag may contain a dead mouse.
　　　　You take out a stubby pencil and look at it as if this puzzling thing came from a different planet.
　　　　You blow a bubble; as you do, the bubble gum gets stuck on your nose. Trying to remove it, your fingers, and even your pencil, get stuck. You fight as if you were a fly caught in a spider's net.

The magic *if* is especially provocative when applied to inanimate objects, as you'll see from the examples following this situation: A group of students reacts to a lecture in their individual ways. (Tape two to three minutes of a history lecture.)

Group 1 finds the lecture fascinating.
Group 2 is bored.
Group 3 finds the lecture uninteresting but listens intently, since they
  know they have to write a report about the discussed subject.

Group 1: Listen to the lecture with rapt attention, as if you were a glittering chandelier. Your eyes sparkle, you smile, you sit erect, and your head is held high.
Group 2: Listen to the lecture as if you were a soft, rotting orange. Your shoulders are relaxed, there is a feeling of bland smoothness on your face, and your head feels as heavy as if it were filled with nothing but pulp.
Group 3: Listen to the lecture as if you were a dried-out prune. Your shoulders cave in; you cross your arms in front of your chest. You feel yourself as tight and tense as if your intestines were prune pits.

Tips *to Help the Very Young Child*

After you have told your group the story of the "Three Little Pigs," announce that they are to perform it. Since the magic *if* heavily depends upon posture, gait, and body movements, you will work with them on these areas.

Characters: Miss Wiggly: Move as if you were to wear a pretty party dress. You are very proud of this dress.

Oscar Piggy: Move around as quickly as if you were on roller skates, or as if you were to ride your tricycle.

Elmo Piggy: Move as if you were to wear shoes that are too small and too tight for you. Move as if your feet hurt you.

Wolf: Move as if you were to wear soft felt slippers. You do not want to draw any attention to yourself.

Scene: *In front of Oscar Piggy's brick house. Busily he finishes building it.*

124...... Teaching a Young Actor

Provide your group with cardboard boxes of various sizes.

Miss Wiggly, carrying a parasol and happily swinging a dainty purse, prances on stage. She stops in front of Oscar Piggy's house.

MISS WIGGLY: Hi, Oscar. Still busy building your brick house?

Without stopping in his work, Oscar Piggy nods.

OSCAR PIGGY: Yes, I got your call. Sorry about what happened to your house.

MISS WIGGLY: Yes, we had a real shock. (*She turns and calls*) Elmo, where are you? Hurry up.

ELMO PIGGY *(Off-stage):* Coming. Coming.

MISS WIGGLY: Hurry up. (*She turns to Oscar*) It was terrible when the wolf blew down our house.

OSCAR PIGGY: I told you to build a sturdy brick house.

MISS WIGGLY *(Shrugs):* Well . . .

Elmo Piggy, struggling with two heavy suitcases, enters. He sets the suitcases down.

OSCAR PIGGY: Hello, Elmo.

ELMO PIGGY: Hello, Oscar. Thanks for inviting us to stay with you for a while.

Elmo wipes his brow, then, picking up the suitcases, he moans.

ELMO PIGGY: Wiggly, the suitcases weigh a ton. Did you pack the kitchen sink?

MISS WIGGLY: No, of course not. I packed my clothes and shoes and a few toys. Get the suitcases into the house.

All of a sudden Oscar Piggy stops working; he listens.

OSCAR PIGGY: The wolf is here.

Miss Wiggly screams; for a moment all three pigs stand frozen, all looking at the silent, slowly approaching wolf. But then Oscar pushes Elmo Piggy and Miss Wiggly into the house.

OSCAR PIGGY: Hurry. Hurry . . .

While the pigs hide in the house (behind the cardboard boxes), the wolf stops in front of the house.

WOLF: I'm the big bad wolf. Come out, you three little piggies.

OSCAR PIGGY: Go away.

ELMO PIGGY: I'll crush you with my suitcases.

MISS WIGGLY: I'll hit you with my umbrella.

The wolf laughs loudly.

WOLF: You come out. Right now. Or I'll huff and puff and blow your house down.

OSCAR PIGGY: Try it.

WOLF: All right. Here goes.

The wolf takes a few steps back, then, as if blowing up a balloon, he takes a deep breath and tries to blow down the house, but fails.

OSCAR PIGGY: See, my house is sturdy. You cannot blow it down.

WOLF: That was just a little blow. Just wait. Here it goes again.

The wolf takes a deeper breath, and again he fails. The three pigs cheer.

WOLF: You haven't seen anything yet.

The wolf tries again and again. He becomes dizzy and starts to weave back and forth, trying to take deeper and deeper breaths. Finally giving up, he slinks away. The three pigs hug each other, then run out of the house and dance around.

ALL: The wolf is gone, the wolf is gone, he'll never bother us again.

MISS WIGGLY: Thank you, Oscar, for building such a sturdy brick house.

ELMO PIGGY: Thanks for being such a good friend.

SESSION 9

Hand and Arm Movements

It is a common mistake among actors to disregard the special power inherent in hands and arms. These actors use either strong gestures that distract from their verbal expression or, even worse, hand movements to emphasize their lines.

Once inappropriate hand movements have become habitual, it is difficult to overcome the compulsion to use them, which may jeopardize otherwise good acting skills. It is therefore important to acquaint children early with the fact that hand and arm movements have a vocabulary of their own. All you need is a tabletop and gloves:

Happy hands
Angry hands
Caressing hands
Grabbing hands
Hesitant hands
Afraid hands
Vain hands

Hands that become a flower
Hands that become a spider
Hands that become a ball
Hands that become a piece of jewelry
Hands that become a toy

Tips *to Help the Very Young Child*

A number of the preceding exercises can be fun and educational for younger children. If any of your students show frustration about hand exercises, you may introduce a very simple one, People on the Bus, and have them act out the following movement:

> The door opens (both hands to the side)
> The door closes (hands close)
> The wheels go round and round (rotating hand motion)
> There is Grandma on the bus; she knits (knitting movement)
> There is Dad, who reads a newspaper (spread hands)
> There is Billy, who cannot wait to get to school (drum hands on knees)
> The wheels go round and round (rotating hand movements)

With hand exercises, the instructions for the very young child have ended. Part 5, "Method Acting Techniques," is too complicated for the very young child. The juxtaposition of making real what is not reality is too confusing for any young child.

PART FIVE

Method Acting Techniques

Method acting, also called the *Stanislavsky system,* goes back to a series of acting exercises pioneered by the Russian actor Konstantin Stanislavsky (1868– 1938). His training at the Paris Conservatory (1887) gave him an intense dislike for the then prevailing acting style of declamation and bathos. In 1888 he founded the Society of Art and Literature where, experimenting with his "system of inner truth and spiritual realism," he directed a group of amateur actors. Later, with Vladimir Danchenko, he founded the Moscow Art Theater that made Anton Chekhov and Maxim Gorky famous.

Some of Stanislavsky's techniques (remember, these were created to overcome a stilted acting style) today seem old-fashioned and rather amateurish. The majority, however, have become standard acting tools. Most of us do not recognize them as a "system" and therefore do not attribute them to Stanislavsky, the greatest of all pioneers in the acting field.

Without any doubt, Stanislavsky's most valuable contribution was his insistence upon a character's goal, that is, the contention that an actor must forget about emotions altogether and concentrate on whatever the character wants to achieve. Some of his provocative discoveries that now form the basis of most acting techniques are

Physical actions
The magic *if*
The application of the actor's own personality
The realistic handling of props

Later, Lee Strasberg continued and expanded Stanislavsky's traditions during his work at the Actors Studio in New York. He stressed the importance of sense memories, and an acting style known as the *method* became not only the source of some of the most innovative acting performances seen on the American stage and screen but also the base from which a number of stars and countless talented but less-known actors created performances of seemingly effortless naturalism.

As the method became exceedingly popular and more and more actors and wannabes tried to absorb its message either by reading about it or by attending seminars and workshops conducted by coaches far removed from the original source, something detrimental happened. Based on the affirmation of Freud's psychological theory of the guiding force of the subconscious, a self-absorbed acting style emerged, concentrating on a supposedly "rich" but in actuality overworked "inner life." This style, depending on unmotivated pauses, unclear emotions, mumbled lines, and distracting overhandling of props, was far removed from Stanislavsky's simplicity and Strasberg's spontaneity, and—in its self-absorption—contradicted Stanislavsky's demand that "an actor's emotions are worthless unless they reach the audience." This self-absorbed acting style depended heavily on "affective memory"—one of Stanislavsky's less effective acting techniques—a tool of emotional recall. Affective memory goes back to an emotionally traumatic or elating incident that really happened.

Ask a group of actors what *method* is, and affective memory will most likely be their first response. Then, after they have pondered your question, someone will say that method acting means you have to bring strongly felt emotions to the part; you have to "become the character."

These statements plainly illustrate what method is *not*. Affective memory, even though once strongly advocated by Stanislavsky, has proven ineffective in the long run. As any psychologist will tell you, even the most traumatic or exhilarating experience becomes ineffective if recalled repeatedly. To recall a traumatic experience over a period of time makes it less painful, so that the person confronting such an experience repeatedly will gradually cleanse himself or herself of its impact.

So what is method acting? As Stanislavsky put it, method acting is a "conscious means to the subconscious" (the actor's true emotions). In this respect, method acting encourages an actor to use his or her own personality, but it does not condone the glorification of that personality.

Method acting guides the actor away from both phony and self-centered emotional expression. It enables the actor to approach and control the seemingly uncontrollable realm of emotions through the application of goals, physical actions, and sense memories. (Please do not confuse sense memory, which will be explained later on, with affective memory.)

Method acting, since it demands the actor's attention from moment to moment, keeps the actor from

Anticipating what will happen next
Criticizing his/her performance while performing
Being preoccupied with whether the casting director, director, or audience will be impressed with his/her performance

Method acting keeps the actor concentrated on his or her performance and in this way keeps a performance honest and spontaneous. It teaches the actor that "inspiration" does not exist but, in the words of Stanislavsky, is the "fruit of long and arduous labor."

By demanding the actor's concentration on "truthful detail," method acting keeps the actor from giving a vague and therefore clichéd performance.

Granted, only certain aspects of the *method* are suitable for a child actor's maturity range. These, however, are necessary acting tools for any child who wishes to make acting his or her career. In this section you will become acquainted with the following method acting techniques:

Character's inner core (attitude)
Personal object
Sense memory
Images
Rhythm—Speed

SESSION 1

Character's Inner Core (Attitude)

Introduce your students to what is termed a character's inner core (inner core pertains to a character's attitude about himself/herself and others). Here are a few examples:

Playful
Bossy
Shy
Self-assured
Depressed
Nervous
Indecisive
Prying

This list will confuse your students; after all, these attributes might seem to belong to the *to be* category—to be playful, to be bossy—which, as your students have learned, cannot be portrayed. Explain to your students that the list pertains to a character's attitude *only*, and that an attitude can be portrayed only after a goal, appropriate to the situation to be explored, has been established. Remind them not to confuse attitude with goal or to confuse attitude with emotion; after all, emotion results from the goal's satisfaction or frustration.

The character type list refers to a character's basic attitude (his/her inner core). Every one of your students knows someone who fits right into your list.

Explain that a character's attitude is an important clue as the actor proceeds to flesh out the character he or she will portray. Fleshing out a character means that the actor's body becomes fully involved in the creation of a character; that is, the main goal has to be translated into physical actions. Here are a few examples that make it easier to explain this seemingly complicated process:

Character Attitude	Main Goal	Physical Action
Prying	I want to stick my nose in other people's business.	Head area: I smell something burning.
		Body area: I get my *hands* ready to *search* for hidden things.
Nervous	I want to get a situation over with.	Head area: I *hear* a telephone ring incessantly.
		Body area: Ants *crawl* in the palms of your hands.

Character Attitude	Main Goal	Physical Action
Self-assured	I want to control my environment.	Head area: I *feel* warm wind on my face.
		Body area: I walk as erect as if I were wearing a knight's armor.
Playful	I want to tease everyone.	Head area: I *blow* bubble gum.
		Body area: I *walk* on pink clouds.
Indecisive	I do not want to make any decision.	Head area: My eyes are unfocused.
		Body area: My hands *touch* soft cotton balls.

Ask your students to perform the listed exercises or, if they desire, create exercises of their own. Do not permit the children to use any real props; limit them to imaginary ones.

Your next step is to ask each student to pick a character attitude from the line and to add a situation to it:

You show a new student around school.

You are getting ready for an interview (TV or movie).

You have to admit to your parents that your report card leaves much to be desired.

You surprise your parents with a great report card.

You have to entertain a boring relative.

You tell a friend about your wonderful trip to Disneyland.

Do not expect any exciting performances, and be aware that your students do feel uncomfortable as they try to portray a character's inner core (attitude). Tell your students not to worry: Method exercises will help them to execute effective (and believable) characterization.

S E S S I O N   2

Personal Object

It might be a good idea to explain method acting to your students like this: "Today we'll start something new. It is an acting technique called method acting. Method acting is lots of fun and helpful for adult and child actors. It helps you express emotions easily. I bet it has happened to you: maybe on an acting job or in a school play when you had to portray an emotion you never felt before."

Ask your students to tell you about such situations. After you have given them sufficient time to discuss this topic, zoom in on one of these incidents. "Mary Ann, you had to play a part in which you were supposed to be afraid of a dog. But you love dogs. You own two dogs and you enjoy playing with them."

"Yes," Mary Ann agrees, "I know I did not do a very good job acting afraid."

"Right, you acted afraid, but you were not afraid at all."

Mary Ann nods.

"So how about thinking of something you are really afraid of?"

Mary Ann takes a long time to think about your question. Finally she says, "I guess it would have to be a tarantula. My cousin has one for a pet." She shudders. "It is big, and so . . . creepy-crawly."

"Would you be afraid to touch it?"

Again Mary Ann shudders. "I would never, ever touch that spider."

"I understand," Timmy exclaims happily. "Mary Ann should have imagined the dog to be a tarantula. Hey, that's neat."

"You are almost right, but not quite. Mary Ann should not have imagined the tarantula, she should have actually seen it."

Timmy, never giving up easily, shakes his head. "But how can she *see* a tarantula if it is not really there?"

"Simple. Mary Ann makes something real that is not real, and she knows it is not real. This is called sense memory, one of the method acting techniques."

Give the children a little time to absorb this strange-sounding statement before you continue: "Making something real that is not real is less difficult than you think." Ask the children to tell you about their favorite games. Laura will remember the wonderful prom she and her friends made up for their Barbie and Ken dolls; Timmy remembers the rainy day when an old trunk he discovered in his grandmother's attic turned into a spaceship that transported him and his brother to the moon; and Mary Ann cannot wait to tell you about the fun she had when the dishwasher became the dashboard of a bus; kitchen chairs were passenger seats occupied by friends, dolls, and stuffed animals; and she (the bus driver) took them on a trip to San Francisco.

Ask your group, "How real were these games?"

"Very real."

"But regardless how real the situations were, you still knew they were make-believe. The same holds true for acting—you make something real that is not real."

(Children are so much closer than adults are to their fantasies that it will be fairly easy for them to accept your contentions. It is far more difficult to convince adult actors of the effectiveness of make-believe.)

And you continue: "Mary Ann, in order to show real fear, not acted fear, should have seen the tarantula creeping toward her, the very moment she was to touch the dog. Let me repeat: Mary Ann should have seen the tarantula, not imagined it."

"The exercise you practiced is called a personal object exercise in method acting." Quickly remind your students of the make-believe exercises they learned when they began this acting course. Make certain that your group remembers them before you go on:

Pick an object you use every day; it may be your toothbrush, milk mug, or a pencil.

Close your eyes and see the object suspended in front of you. Keeping your eyes closed, take a good look at this object:

Determine its shape.

Determine its color or colors.

Take plenty of time to *see* your object.

Once your object has become "somewhat real," lift your hands up to the object, and, keeping your eyes closed, explore it with your fingertips:

Is it smooth?

Is it rough?

Does it have nooks and crannies?
Does it have sharp edges or a smooth surface?

After your students have explored the object, tell them, "Let the object fly away, and open your eyes." Then ask, "How real did your objects become?" You will be pleasantly surprised by the number of students who experienced the reality of the make-believe object:

I was ready to brush my teeth.
I saw my pencil; it needed to be sharpened.
I wanted to take a sip of milk.

Practice a couple more personal object exercises before you move on. Now let's go back to the character's inner core exercise of Session 1. As your students choose a character type to portray, add one of the following short speeches and watch your students have fun.
These are some sample speeches:

Prying. I really want to know what Marsha and Bill are talking about. Are they talking about me? I have to find out.

Nervous. I have no idea what to write about, and my essay is due tomorrow. Why did I procrastinate so long? Now I won't have time to do all the research I was supposed to do.

Self-assured. (Give a little pep talk to your friends) Come on, you can do it. If we all dig in we'll have this room spanking clean by the time the parent-teacher meeting starts.

Playful. (Hold both hands behind your back) You have no idea what I bought for your birthday. It is something you've wanted for a long time. Now guess in which hand am I holding the gift.

Indecisive. I really ought to go to the bookstore and buy some textbooks. But the books are so expensive, and I'm saving up for a new bike. Well, I might go to the library to read the books there. But it's so far to the library, and the library is not open every day. I really should buy the books . . . so what shall I do?

Announce that each exercise will have to be done twice. First, each student has to concentrate on the physical actions suggested under "head area," followed by the physical actions suggested under "body area." Advise your students that the physical actions have to be established before they speak the lines:

Really *smell* something burning.
Really *feel* ants crawling in the palms of your hands.
Really *hear* the telephone ring.

S E S S I O N   3

Sense Memory (I)

"Last session," you begin, "you had your first glimpse of a method acting exercise called sense memory. Sense memories do not permit the actor to 'act' an emotion. As you, the actor, have to concentrate on a physical action caused by a sense memory, you are able to express the character's appropriate emotion easily, because you did not focus on the emotion but on an object that caused the emotion easily."

Sense memories are based on the senses:

Touch
Smell
Taste
Sight
Sound

Make certain that your students understand the purpose of sense memories. For instance, one may use the taste of chocolate to express delight about a situation but not to talk about Aunt Emma's delicious chocolate cake. Or one may choose the smell of garbage to express a character's frustration about a situation but not if a scene requires that the actor empty a garbage pail.

Remind your group of the previous exercise, where they had to smell something burning, feel ants crawling over their hands, and blow bubbles. All these sensations, as you will remember, caused certain emotions. You were happy blowing bubbles, nervous as you felt the ants in your hands, and apprehensive as you smelled something burning. These sense memories are not connected *directly* with the emotions the character was supposed to express. (For instance, don't apply bubble blowing to that particular physical activity only but to any moment when your character is happy.)

The first sense memory your group will learn is touch. Ask your students to:

> Close your eyes and select a personal object, something you like to
> touch: a kitten, a puppy, a doll, your favorite book, your roller skates.
> Once you have established the personal object, count to ten.
> Keep the personal object going and recite a nursery rhyme.

It is important that you give each child the opportunity to select his or her favorite object; do not make things easy for them by suggesting one general personal object for all. Don't forget, method acting aims toward individual expression. Laura loves her kitten; therefore, Timmy's personal object, his roller skates, does not mean anything to her, while Mary Ann, who collects dolls, is not affected by Laura's beloved kitten. The children *must* select personal objects that mean something to them.

Do not push your students to show emotions. Honest emotions that are caused by sense memories cannot be forced. On the other hand, do not permit any of the children to show an emotion they do not feel. Leave the children pretty much to their own devices, and you will be surprised by the variation of honestly felt emotions breaking through.

Follow up with three more sense memory exercises:

1. Touch something you love (a kitten, a doll, a puppy).

2. Touch something you are very proud of (a trophy you have won, your favorite outfit, your new bike, the terrific essay you wrote).

3. Touch something you admire but are hesitant to touch (an expensive piece of jewelry, your mother's best china dish, a crystal goblet, butterfly wings).

Discuss with your students the emotions they felt while practicing the sense memory exercises.

Exercise 1: evoked the emotion of caring and protecting and preserving.

Exercise 2: evoked the emotion of pride in possession.

Exercise 3: evoked the emotion of worried pride.

Point out the different personal objects used in the various touch sense memories. Each object evoked a differently shaded emotion, even though all personal objects caused positive emotions. Because of the shading, sense memory personal objects should not be chosen arbitrarily but must fit

The character type (inner core) to be portrayed
The situation encountered
The goal selected

Agreed, this technique may sound a little too complicated for your child actors, but once they have performed two short monologues illustrating what you are talking about, they will grasp the idea.

In the following monologue, Rita/Ralph is on the telephone telling his or her best friend the terrific news that he or she has been cast for the lead in a TV show.

RITA/RALPH: You won't believe my good news. You remember last week I auditioned for this TV show? When I arrived at the casting office, I almost left. There were so many kids there and they all had terrific pictures. I kind of stole a glance at some of the résumés—boy oh boy, did they have great credits. But I told myself that I had to go through with the audition. Yes . . . I'm getting to my good news. Well, I had a callback, and you know how it is, I didn't hear a word for several days, and then bingo, my agent called—I got the job. Yes, I got the job! I can't tell you how happy I am, but, honestly, I'm worried, I never played a lead before. I hope I don't mess up. . . .

Supply your students with a prop telephone and have them perform the monologue four times:

Apply Exercise 1: Evoke the emotion of caring and preserving (pet a puppy or kitten).

Apply Exercise 2: Evoke the emotion of pride in possession (look at your favorite toy).

Apply Exercise 3: Evoke the emotion of worried pride (carry your mother's prized crystal bowl).

Finally, integrate all three sense memories (at the appropriate segments) throughout the monologue.

Be aware that your students will no longer *perform* but *live* the given text. Their emotions—clearly but simply expressed—will affect you. And this is what good acting is all about.

Give the children enough time to congratulate themselves and each other on their excellent performances and let them express their delight about how easy sense memories are to use, but bring them down to earth by reminding them that sense memories should not be used for positive emotions only, but for negative emotions as well.

After this advice, you will, of course, continue to work on touch. And again, as during the previous (positive) touch exercise, take time to discuss with your group what kinds of things they are afraid to touch. Permit each child to choose a touch object (snake, spider, etc.) of his or her own and practice the negative touch exercise the same way as you worked on the positive touch exercise.

Integrate three sense memories as appropriate to the different segments in the following monologue: Again, as in the previous monologue, Rita/Ralph is on the phone talking to her/his best friend. Rita/Ralph knows that one of her/his friends has invented a "surefire" method of cheating during tests. She/he feels the homeroom teacher ought to be notified about this student's dishonesty. But—and this is the crux of the problem—Ralph/Rita does not want to squeal on the friend.

RITA/RALPH: You know, I've thought it over, and I really don't know what to do. What Chuck does is wrong. You and I found out, and we know we ought to stop him—he gets good grades but he doesn't learn a thing. He only hurts himself. I really think we should tell our homeroom teacher. Don't you agree? Really, what he does is disgusting. But, you know, I'm afraid to tell on him. The other kids will call us snitches. And how about Chuck—you know how angry he gets. He might never speak to us again.

Sense Memory (II)

Today, following the previously established format, you'll work on the sense memories of sight and sound.

Positive Sight
See something that makes you calm and happy (evening sky over a mountaintop, a meadow dotted with flowers) to evoke the emotion of contentment and happiness.

See something that makes you proud (an A on an essay you worked very hard on, your new bike you have saved a long time for, the present you've bought for your mother with money you've earned) to evoke the emotion of excited pride.

See something that makes you laugh (a funny clown, a great cartoon) to evoke the emotion of hilarity.

Characters: B (Bart/Beth)
C (Charles/Colette)
S (Sam/Sally)
T (Tim/Tina)

Scene: *Christmas morning.*

Children show their presents to each other.

B: Look, look what I found . . . a kitten . . . a real live kitten. Isn't it sweet? How soft. How cuddly.

S: Please let me hold it.

B: Sure, but be careful; don't hurt it.

S: What are you going to call it?

B: Fluffy. Its fur is so soft.

S: Fluffy? I don't like it. How about . . . Emerald? Look, its eyes look like Mother's ring.

C comes by.

S: Show me what you've got.

B takes kitten back from S, cuddles kitten.

B: Yes, show us.

C: You won't believe it—I've got Rollerblades. Father said no way when I asked for them, but here they are. I can't wait to try them out.

S picks up a package and pulls out a sweater.

S: And look at my Christmas present—a sweater. Come on, touch it, it's as soft as the kitten.

B: And I've got more things. I've got books.

T: Tapes . . .

S: Games . . .

T: But best of all, we have each other and we can spend Christmas together.

They all hug.

> *Negative Sight*
> See something that makes you angry (a small child who has been
> punished unnecessarily, a hurt puppy or kitten) to evoke the emotion
> of anger.

See something that makes you sad (you have worked diligently for a test only to be rewarded with a D) to evoke the emotion of puzzled sadness.

See something that makes you afraid (a mouse, a cockroach, a vicious dog) that evokes the emotion of fear.

The negative sight sense memories in the following scene, "No Help," apply for M only.

Characters: M (Mel/Martha)
              N (Norm/Nettie)

N is busily doing his/her homework, as M softly knocks.

N: Come in.

M: Sorry to disturb you; I know you're busy with your homework.

N: Get to the point.

M: I need some help with math.

N: Forget it.

M: I have a test tomorrow, and if I don't get a C, I won't pass.

N: That's none of my concern, so stop bothering me.

M: Listen, you've got to help me. You owe me. Remember I quizzed you for your history test.

N: That was weeks ago. That history test *is* history.

M: All right, be selfish.

After your group has performed the scenes based on positive and negative sight sense memories, continue with the sense memory of sound.

Positive Sound
Hear something that makes you calm (the sound of rain on treetops, a song) to evoke the emotion of calm happiness.

Hear something that makes you so happy you could cry (you hear the voice of a friend you have not seen for a long time) to evoke the emotion of happiness mixed with sadness.

Hear something that makes you jump with joy (your favorite song, the sound of the Disneyland marching band) to evoke the emotion of extreme happiness.

Supply your students with a tape recorder to record a diary and have them integrate sight sense memories that will induce the previously listed emotional responses of happiness at the appropriate segments of the monologue:

Dear Diary: Today is my first day of vacation. I'm so happy I want to jump up and down, I want to hug everyone in sight—my mother, my little sister, Mouser the resident hotel cat, even Aunt Edith, with whom I usually do not see eye to eye. Yesterday Mother and I loaded the car and picked up Aunt Edith and drove all the way to Yosemite Park. It is simply wonderful here. From our balcony I can look upon a meadow bordered by huge trees, and in the distance I can see the mountains. The birds are tame enough to pick bread crumbs off the guests' hands, and at dusk deer and their young come close to the hotel. But best of all, day after tomorrow we'll drive to San Francisco to meet Dad. For the past three months he has been on active duty with the navy in the Pacific. Finally he's coming home. I cannot wait to see him.

Negative Sound
Hear something that frustrates you (chalk scraping across a blackboard, the sound of a "boom box") to evoke the emotion of frustration.

Hear something that makes you freeze with fear (the sound of a door opening when you are alone at home, the rattle of a rattlesnake) to evoke an emotion of fear, strong enough to make it impossible for you to move.

Hear something that makes you sad (a song, a voice that evokes the emotion of sadness deep enough to make you cry).

Follow up with a monologue that employs the appropriate sense memories. Your uncle has given you an original Mickey Mouse watch for your birthday. One afternoon, getting ready to visit your uncle and aunt, you decide to wear the watch, only it is not in its case. You start looking for it. This is the type of monologue that requires the students to choose the goal of wanting to gain control over a situation. To evoke the appropriate emotions, encourage children to use negative sound sense memories of *their own choosing,* not necessarily the ones given in the list. Since this monologue requires the combination of definite physical actions and verbal expressions all based on emotional responses, it is somewhat difficult to perform. For this reason sense memories have been suggested at the appropriate segment.

> Where is my watch? I know I put it back into its case yesterday. I came home from school and before I did the dishes I put my watch away. *(Sound sense memory that makes you want to climb a wall)* All right, get a hold of yourself; the watch must be somewhere. If I calm down I'll remember where I put it. Maybe I put it with my school books . . . no, nothing here. I couldn't have dropped it into the laundry basket . . . well, I did throw my T-shirt into the laundry basket, and Mom did the laundry this morning. *(Sound sense memory that makes you freeze with fear)* — Oh no, my watch is ruined. How can I explain this to Uncle Bill? How can I explain I was careless with a gift he spent so much thought and money on? What shall I do? What shall I do? I liked that watch. I was so proud of it. *(Sound sense memory that makes you sad)*
>
> *All of a sudden you look down. Your body tenses, then it relaxes as you pick up the watch that had been hidden on a table next to your school books. You pick up the watch. (Sound sense memory that makes you happy)*
>
> What is this? I can't believe it. Here is my watch *(Sound sense memory that makes you calm)* right next to my school books. I've found my watch!

SESSION 5

Sense Memory (III)

Positive Taste
Taste something you really like to eat (your favorite food) that evokes the emotion of joy.

You are ravenously hungry, and finally after what seems an eternity you get some food, to evoke the emotion of gratitude.

Taste a cool drink of water after you have been playing a vigorous game of tennis, to evoke the emotion of deep satisfaction.

In the following scene, "The Callboard," two members of the drama club are standing in front of the callboard, congratulating one another for having been cast in the school play.

Characters: Lynn
              Ed

ED: Congratulations.

LYNN: Congratulations to you.

ED: We've made it. We've got the parts we wanted.

Taste that evokes the emotion of joy.

LYNN: I cannot believe it, I simply cannot believe it. You know, Marsha read so well in the audition, I was certain she'd get the part of the mean stepmother.

ED: I thought I had no chance . . . and here I have been cast for Lucifer the cat. Boy, will I have fun. Meow-Meeeeooooouuuuuuuw.

Taste that evokes the emotion of gratitude.

ED: But we'll have to work hard to show our teacher we deserve these terrific roles.

LYNN: It will be fun to learn lines, to go to rehearsals, to meet new friends, to perform on the stage.

Taste that evokes the emotion of deep satisfaction.

ED: Boy, are we lucky.

Negative Taste
Taste something that makes you gag (any food you cannot stand) to evoke the *physical* feeling of nausea.

Taste something that draws your mouth together (bite into a lemon) to evoke the feeling of strong dislike.

Taste something that makes your body shake with disgust (a bitter health tea, a rotten peach, a worm in an apple) to evoke the feeling of repulsion.

Again the two friends Ed and Lynn peruse the callboard. They have been cast for roles they detest. Ed has been cast as Lucifer the cat, and Lynn was cast for the role of the wicked stepmother. Ed had hoped to be Prince Charming, and Lynn had dreamed of the glamorous ball gown she would wear as Cinderella.

Taste that evokes physical nausea.

ED: Look at that. She cast me for Lucifer. That's sick. She needs to have her head examined. I would have been perfect for Prince Charming.

LYNN: Stop your bellyaching. You have nothing to complain about.

ED: Ha! I have to wear that hot, smelly, ugly cat outfit.

LYNN: And how about me? She cast me as the wicked stepmother. I'll have to wear padding, and I have to waddle across the stage. I hope none of my friends will come to see that dumb play.

Taste that evokes a feeling of strong dislike.

ED: *And* we'll have to go to rehearsals.

LYNN: Many rehearsals.

ED: Yeah, and she's so picky, she insists that we know our lines.

Taste that evokes a feeling of repulsion.

ED: We'll miss out on so many things because of those silly rehearsals.

LYNN: We miss out on tennis . . .

ED: Swimming . . .

LYNN: Oh no, I just remembered . . . even worse. Have you forgotten? We were supposed to go to New York on vacation.

ED: Great Scott, you're right. Rehearsals are called during vacation.

LYNN: Fate has hit us a blow.

ED: Life couldn't be worse.

Some of your students, even you, might question the necessity of practicing the given series of sense memories. After all, since all of them cause positive or negative emotional expressions, why not use one type of sense memory only? Interestingly enough, different senses used for sense memories change and color the actor's emotional expression. Why not test this by running one of the practice scenes through different sense memories (touch, taste, smell, sight, sound)? You will be surprised at the difference in expressions.

All through the previous session your group became more natural in the way they expressed emotions and were more in tune with their open feelings. They are now less inclined to "act" or show emotions they do not feel. In short, your students are now on their way to becoming effective actors.

SESSION 6

Images (I)

Sense memories, since they employ the five senses, are based on actualities — things you can taste, smell, touch, hear, and see. (Taste chocolate, smell a flower, touch a silk dress, hear music, see the ocean.) *Images,* on the other hand, are based on sensations that originate in your body and radiate from there through your body. Images (as opposed to sense memories, which are objects placed outside your body) are objects placed within your body.

Generally, images should be used for characterizations, all-encompassing emotions, or for emotions the actor has *not* experienced in life. We have only a relatively small number of images at our disposal, a fact that should encourage your students to search for new ones:

Boiling teakettle in your stomach
Soap bubbles in your eyes and mouth
Sunshine radiating from your stomach to your eyes and mouth
Malevolent rays (or daggers) in your eyes
A steel plate reaching from your neck down your spine
Your spine as a clump of ice

Admittedly, these image exercises, though fun to do, take a bit of practice. All through the practice session, remind your group that an *image must be based on a goal.*

Goal: I want to keep my anger under control.

Emotion: Anger that becomes more violent as you try to control it.

Image: You carry a teakettle filled with boiling water in your stomach. This teakettle is ready to explode (your anger); only if you press both your hands on the lid will you keep the kettle from exploding.

Exercise: Physically press both hands down, first while counting to ten, then while reciting a nursery rhyme.

Repeat this exercise (counting and reciting a nursery rhyme) while feeling the physical hand movement.

Body Condition: Negative 5

Now have your students work through the practice scene "The Ruined Sweater."

Characters: O (Oscar/Opal)
             G (Gerry/Gertrude)

Scene: *Oscar/Opal accuses Gerry/Gertrude of not only having swiped his/her best sweater but also of having it "decorated" with paint spots.*

O: I'm telling you, in the future don't even *think* about taking anything of mine.

G: I did not take your dumb sweater, I borrowed it.

O: You took my sweater. You swiped it.

G: Okay, okay, so I took your sweater. I was in a rush. I had to go back to school to work on the sets for our school play. You know how cold it is backstage.

O: Aha! That's how the paint spots got on it. What do you have to say to that?

G: Don't make a federal case out of a few little dots.

O: Dots? These spots are bigger than Lake Michigan.

G: So I'll take your precious possession to the dry cleaners.

O: I already did. No one can clean my sweater.

Finally the teakettle boils over. O throws the sweater at G.

O: Take it and keep it.

G: Thanks. I'll wear it for rehearsal tonight. I'll start a new fashion.

Soap Bubbles

Goal: I want to express my love of life.

Emotion: Happiness, radiating through your eyes and from your smile, flows through your body.

Image: Iridescent, shiny soap bubbles tumble in your stomach, and from there radiate to your eyes, mouth, and smile.

Exercise: See bubbles, count to ten. See bubbles, recite nursery rhyme.

Body Condition: Positive 5

Scene: *You have worked hard in school and have been rewarded with the very best report card you ever had. Waving your report card, you storm into your house.*

Mom! Dad! Look! Look at this! I got an A in math, and a B in biology. I worked so hard, but I never dreamed I'd get an A in math. And in most of my other subjects I have Bs. . . . and only one C. I'm so—happy—happy—happy—

S E S S I O N   7

Images II

Goal: I want to comfort and rescue.

Emotion: You feel strong compassion and a sense of commitment to another.

Image: You carry sunshine in your solar plexus (stomach). Sunshine radiates through your eyes, mouth, and hands.

Exercise: Feel sunshine, count to ten. Feel sunshine and recite a nursery rhyme.

Body Condition: Positive 2

In the following scene, your little sister/brother has accidentally broken an expensive vase. You comfort him/her.

YOU: I know you didn't do it on purpose.

BROTHER/SISTER: I didn't see it. I was reaching for the juice pitcher . . .

YOU: And there it was. I understand. Don't cry.

Little Brother/Sister keeps on sniffling. You hand him/her some tissue.

BROTHER/SISTER: I'm so afraid Mom will be angry.

YOU: No, she won't. I'll tell her how it happened. Everything will be okay.

BROTHER/SISTER: Sure?

YOU: Sure.

Little Brother/Sister hugs you. You hug him/her back.

BROTHER/SISTER: I love you.

YOU: I love you, too.

Malevolent Rays/Daggers

Goal: I want to destroy.

Emotion: You have to destroy everything that stands in your way.

Image: Rays (or daggers) emerge from your solar plexus and radiate from there to your eyes, mouth, and hands.

Exercise: Feel rays and count to ten. Feel rays and recite nursery rhyme.

Body Condition: Negative 3

In the following scene, the wicked queen, Snow White's stepmother, talks to her mirror.

Characters: Queen
            Mirror

QUEEN: Mirror, mirror, on the wall, who is the fairest of them all?

MIRROR: You were, my queen, but now Snow White is the fairest of them all.

QUEEN: Don't lie, mirror. You know Snow White is dead. The hunter, upon my command, killed her.

MIRROR: I beg your pardon, my queen, I don't lie. Snow White is alive; she lives over the hills with the seven dwarfs.

QUEEN: Don't ever dare to talk to me again. You hear me? Never ever.

MIRROR: Your wish is my command, my queen.

The Queen starts pacing the room.

QUEEN: I have to do something. I have to destroy Snow White. Ah, I've found the answer. I'll visit that wretched girl. I'll disguise myself as a peddler, and I'll poison Snow White with an apple. No, even better, I will kill her with a poisoned comb.

Images III

Goal: I want to control.

Emotion: Your body and soul have been pressed into an emotional straitjacket.

Image: A steel plate, giving your body a rigid quality, reaches from your neck down your spine.

Exercise: Feel the steel in your body and count to ten. Feel the steel plate in your body and recite a nursery rhyme.

Body Condition: Negative 3

In this scene, Martin/Maggie is the chairperson for the homeroom open house. It is his or her duty to see that the room is spick-and-span and that the various exhibits are displayed attractively. Unfortunately, enjoying a sense of power, Martin/Maggie goes overboard.

Characters: M (Martin/Maggie)
　　　　　　　A (Alan/Annie)
　　　　　　　P (Peter/Penny)
　　　　　　　O (Ollie/Ona)
　　　　　　　R (Rich/Ruth)

M: Well, I can only say our room does not meet the specification set at our meeting yesterday.

A: We worked very hard. I think our classroom looks fine.

M: Not good enough to welcome our parents and friends.

o: We worked very hard. We did our best.

m: I don't think your best is good enough.

M walks to a display.

m: How about the drawings on the wall? Each and every one of them hangs crooked.

p: Don't strain yourself. I'll straighten the drawing out in a jiffy.

M moves on.

m: And look at our exhibit; all the items are labeled wrong.

r: Who cares? I bet no one will take a second look at those dumb stones.

m: Stones? Are you kidding? This is a science exhibit. Read my lips: science exhibit. I want it labeled right.

r: And you read my lips: Get lost.

m: I'm the one in charge, and you are going to do what I ask you to do.

r: All right, if you insist.

m: And now everyone listen up: The floor has to be swept.

R AND A *(In unison):* Come on, the floor is fine.

a: I swept the floor before we tackled the exhibits.

m: I don't care if you've swept the floor with a toothbrush; it has to be done over again.

Spine Has Turned to Ice

Goal: I don't want to be bothered by or with anything. I've shut off my emotions.

Emotion: None.

Image: Your spine has turned to ice, your body is as rigid as your soul.

Exercise: Feel the ice and count to ten. Feel the ice and recite a nursery rhyme.

Body Condition: Negative 1

In the next scene, P asks O to buy a present for their mother, but O refuses to do so.

Characters: P (Peter/Penny)
O (Ossie/Olga)

P: No, I don't think I'll buy a present for Mom. A card will do.

O: Are you out of your mind? Don't you think Mom should get an extra-nice present from you?

P: Why?

O: Have you forgotten how she quizzed you for your history test, and helped with your biology assignment, and did your chores when you were too "busy"?

P: But I'm saving my money to buy a new video recorder, and you know how much they cost.

O: Mom will be hurt.

P: She'll get over it.

O: Get real. Buy a present.

P: Why?

O: Because a present is a token to show her how grateful you are, how much you appreciate her, and how much you love her.

P: A card will do.

S E S S I O N   9

Rhythm and Speed

Begin this session by talking about the difference between *rhythm* and *speed*.

There is a specific rhythm in every one of us. This rhythm controls speech and physical actions as well as thoughts. Some of us are slow in speech and movements, others display a more deliberate approach, and quite a few are tuned in to an increasingly accelerated pace, much in contrast to the ones who—like hummingbirds—flit from task to task or idea to idea.

Permit the children to discover and discuss their own individual rhythm patterns before you help them to beat out the rhythms of

The slow mover
The deliberate mover
The fast mover

After your group has gained some understanding of the various rhythms, point out that verbal expression as well as physical action must correspond to the chosen character's rhythm pattern.

If possible, supply your students with real props (bookcase and books) for the following exercise:

"It is a rainy Sunday afternoon. You had planned to meet your friends at the beach, but now you're stuck at home. On the spur of the moment you have decided to straighten up your bookcase. Have your verbal expression and physical actions correspond to the previously listed rhythm patterns."

You look at the books: "Now how should I do this? Textbooks on the upper shelf, fiction on the middle shelf, or maybe on the lower shelf . . . no, that's where nonfiction ought to be."

You begin rearranging the books, but soon you get distracted: "Now look at that; I had forgotten all about that one. When did I borrow it from Rita? That was quite a while ago. And I never read that book."

You peruse the book; after a while you reluctantly put it aside: "I better return the book tomorrow. Now back to my books. Maybe, just maybe, I should arrange them differently. How about in alphabetical order? No, that won't do."

You look out the window: "Hey, it stopped raining. Maybe I'll call Fred and Mary and we'll go to the mall."

Speed, in comparison, applies to the *tempo* a character chooses to accomplish a task.

Speed level 1 — slow
Speed level 2 — medium
Speed level 3 — fast

Have some boxes and towels ready. Ask your students to fold the towels, place them into a box, and, while observing the speed levels, count to twenty. As soon the children feel secure in speed levels, add the following exercise:

> You are packing a suitcase, but since your favorite TV program is on, you are more interested in it than in your chore.
> (Speed level 1)

> You are packing a suitcase in your usual efficient way. Every so often you glance at the TV.
> (Speed level 2)

> You hurry. You have to catch a plane, and you are late. You give the TV a cursory look only.
> (Speed level 3)

Remind the students that their verbal expressions and physical actions have to correspond with the speed levels while they perform this monologue:

> I'm surely going to miss this show. I better take another pair of shorts along. Oh no, this has a big spot. Well, it doesn't matter, for running around the beach it will do just fine. And I'll need more T-shirts. I sure wish I could watch the show all week . . . but, well—oh yes, and socks, I never take enough socks along. I wish I could find out who wins on today's show. I better pack my sunscreen and beach towels. Too bad I cannot wait for the show to end.

Since so many scenes in movies and TV depend on rhythm and speed, these elements have to flow smoothly and naturally. Don't permit your students to let physical actions and verbal expressions overshadow each other.

PART SIX

Auditioning

Auditioning Techniques

The time has come for your students to be ready to compete. By now some of them have been accepted by agents and will go on auditions for movies, TV shows, and commercials, while others may compete for roles in school plays. Whether the children audition on a professional or amateur level, or whether they audition for a casting director or teacher, each audition has to be taken seriously. Therefore, it is a good idea to present your students with a photocopied list of the do's and do not's of an audition:

Do not be nervous.

Do feel secure in the knowledge that you have prepared yourself to the best of your ability and are *ready* to audition.

Do not primp for the audition.

Do look exactly as natural and vital as your headshot (8 × 10 photo) depicts you.

Do not stiffen as you talk to the casting director/agent. (Many professionals complain that actors (child and adult alike) display the desirable element of "vitality" on their headshots, only to appear shy and "flat" once they audition or interview.)

Do be your natural, outgoing, likable self. Show that you enjoy the interview, that you are proud of yourself and your accomplishments.

Do not try to impress the casting director/agent with an "impressive" reading; in short, do not "act."

Do communicate emotional and intensity levels as you read for a part.

Do not ask yourself: "How does the casting director/teacher want me to read the part?"

Do read the part as you have decided it should be read. After all, it is your own personality that makes you a candidate to be considered for a callback. (Callback means that an actor will be called in again to read.)

Do not search for a character's feeling as you prepare your reading.

Do decide upon a character's goal, and if possible the character's attitude (inner core).

Do not ask your parents to hire an acting coach to work with you if you receive a callback. It may drain your performance of vitality.

Do work on your reading yourself by strengthening what you did well during the first audition.

Do not follow the intensity level set by the casting director/teacher reading opposite you during an audition. These people intentionally keep their responses on a very low, uncommitted level, to get a better idea about your interpretation.

Do keep all your intensity levels and emotional levels as well as sense memories and thoughts as *you* had planned.

Do not be disappointed if, even after a terrific reading, you aren't called back, or after a callback, you aren't cast. There are many conditions beyond your control:
   You might be too young or old.
   You might be too tall or short.
   Your part has been canceled.
   You are blond and they decided on a redhead.
   And so on . . .

Do be proud of your reading, and be happy that you did the best job you could possibly do. If you feel, however, that you could have done better, don't hesitate to go over the areas that need improvement, and be confident in the knowledge that the casting director/teacher remembers a good reading and will call you in again.

S E S S I O N   2

Mock Auditions

I have found *mock auditions* to be a terrific device to help my "agent-bound" students over the first hurdles of interviews and auditions.

Ask one of the older students to sit in as agent/casting director while you work on your group's audition techniques. These are the areas you want your students to pay close attention to:

1. As you walk toward the agent/casting director's desk, smile and make eye contact. Do not look at the floor.

2. Introduce yourself—"Hi, I'm . . ."—and hand him/her your 8 × 10 photo and résumé (make certain that your résumé has been stapled *securely* to your photo).

3. Wait for him/her to extend his/her hand and wait to be invited to sit down.

4. Sit relaxed. Don't fiddle with your hair or clothing.

5. Do not interrupt the agent/casting director while he/she looks at your picture and résumé. If you have a portfolio containing more professional photos, wait patiently until he/she has gone through it.

6. Do not apologize for having little experience in the acting field, and therefore few or no credits. Do not belittle any of your achievements but, without bragging, speak proudly of them.

7. To gain some idea about your personality the agent/casting director

will probably touch on topics such as school, pets, hobbies, or trips you have taken. Don't respond with a shy "Yes," "No," or even worse, "I don't know."

Speak in full sentences.
Be enthusiastic.
Show vitality (very important).
Be yourself; do not project an assumed personality.

8. Once the interview has been concluded, thank the agent/casting director for having taken the time to meet with you.

9. Do not ask, "Will you represent me?" or "Is there any part for me?" Smile, shake the agent/casting director's hand, and, head held high, walk out of the office.

SESSION 3

Tips for Preparing a Reading

Arrive about thirty minutes before your scheduled audition. Sign in at the casting director's office. If you are auditioning for movies and/or TV ask the receptionist for your "sides"; if auditioning for a commercial you will ask for your "copy."

1. Don't search for the character's feeling; instead, establish his/her goal. Admittedly, this is at times impossible to do, since you'll have only one or two printed pages at your disposal. If you cannot find a goal, forget about it and go on.

2. Establish the character's attitude (inner core). Choose an image or sense memory to portray this attitude.

3. Decide on the appropriate emotional levels (positive and negative) and the communication levels (intensity levels).

4. Decide on thoughts. Remember that "thoughts lead to verbal expression."

5. Do not hesitate to jot down this information on your sides or copy.

6. Once you have decided on these items, go outside into the hallway and read the scene aloud. Listen to yourself and remember the following:

Communicate clearly.

Be your own vital and unique self or, if necessary, portray a believable character attitude.

Don't ever act; don't ever show emotions you don't feel. (Use images if you have to portray an emotion you've never experienced.)

7. Before entering the casting director/teacher's office, feel the warm sunshine of confidence radiate from your stomach.

8. As you read, don't ever think, "How does he/she like it? I hope I'll be cast." Instead, go from moment to moment concentrating on the tasks you have to perform (emotional levels, intensity levels, attitude, sense memories, etc.).

9. If, however, you should lose concentration—and it *will happen* every so often—do not panic.

Stop your reading *immediately.*

Permit your mind to go blank.

Let your eyes travel along the straight line of a wall, desk, or book while you say in your mind, "Go back to your task" (your thoughts, intensity or emotional levels, sense memories).

Keep on going.

No one will have noticed the slight hesitation. Chances are that the casting director/teacher took your hesitation as part of the reading. Do not, therefore, apologize for having lost concentration.

10. Have fun. Enjoy showing what you have learned. Be proud of yourself and your craft.

Good luck to all of you.

Practice Audition Scene

The following practice audition scene is called "The Proposal."

Characters: Sonja, a young girl
               Michael, a young landowner

Scene: *1850. The terrace of a country mansion in Russia. It is a hot summer afternoon. Dressed in their Sunday best finery, Sonja and Michael are seated at a well-appointed tea table.*

SONJA: Please, dear neighbor, do join me in another cup of tea.

MICHAEL: Dear lady, have mercy on me, this is my third cup.

SONJA: Nonsense, another cup won't hurt you.

She pours some tea. Her hand shakes and she spills some tea on Michael's coat.

SONJA: How clumsy of me. Forgive me.

MICHAEL: Think nothing of it.

He pulls out his handkerchief. As he helps Sonja to clean his sleeve, their faces almost touch. Highly embarrassed, they move apart.

MICHAEL *(Flustered)*: Dear Sonja, I hope, I pray, that I may address you by your first name. I am so excited.

Abruptly, Michael stops.

SONJA *(Coaxing):* Yes, my dear neighbor . . . my dear Michael . . .

MICHAEL: I've made up my mind . . . *(He stops)* May I have a tiny spoonful of honey for my tea?

SONJA: Most certainly.

She pours some honey into his cup.

SONJA: You came to ask me . . .

MICHAEL: I came to ask you . . .

SONJA: Yes, you came to ask me?

MICHAEL: A raisin or two in my tea would be delightful.

Sonja drops a few raisins into Michael's teacup.

SONJA: But of course.

She moves closer to him.

SONJA: As you were saying . . .

Michael takes her hand.

MICHAEL: Dear Sonja, beloved lady, admired neighbor. I came to ask you
  humbly . . . and . . .

Elena, the maid, swinging a half-plucked chicken by its legs, runs in.

ELENA: Madam, take a good look at this chicken. Cook says it's not plucked
  properly, but by all the saints in the heaven, I did the very best I could.
  Please, I beg you, madam, take a look . . .

SONJA *(Screeches):* Out of my sight, you wretched girl.

Michael, amazed by this outburst, looks at Sonja with concern. Elena curtsies.

ELENA: But madam, Cook told me to—

SONJA: Out of my sight.

Picking up her skirt, Elena runs away. Sonja, all sweetness and light, turns to Michael.

SONJA: You were saying, dear, most admired and respected neighbor.

Michael pulls out his handkerchief and wipes his now profusely perspiring brow. Playing for time, he takes another sip of his tea. Sonja watches him anxiously. Finally she cannot contain herself any longer.

SONJA *(Insistent):* You were saying . . . go ahead, don't be bashful.

Michael becomes increasingly more uncomfortable.

SONJA: Let's stop the idle chitchat and get down to the real reason for your visit. *(Sweetly)* A little birdie told me . . .

All of a sudden Sonja shrieks. Grabbing her napkin, she chases a bee. Michael joins the chase. As he does, he stumbles and lands on his knees in front of Sonja.

Elena, still swinging the plucked chicken, runs in.

ELENA: Madam, Cook says . . .

As she sees Michael Kneeling before Sonja, she cries.

ELENA: Thank you, all saints, thank you. Finally someone proposes to madam. Finally she'll get married. Finally we'll get rid of her. Thank you, saints.

Quickly Sonja grabs Michael's hand.

SONJA: Yes, my beloved Michael, I'll accept your proposal, I will be your obedient . . . your dutiful wife.

Michael knows there is no way out. His future has been cast—in iron.

MICHAEL: Yes, beloved Sonja, let's set a wedding day.

Defeated, Michael nods to Sonja's demands, while Elena swings her chicken joyfully.

ELENA: The chicken has been plucked.

$\mathcal{S}$uggested $\mathbb{R}$eading

BOOKS

Bedrad, Roger L., and Tolch, C. John, eds. *Spotlight on the Child: Studies in the History of American Children's Theater.* Westport, Conn.: Greenwood, 1989.

Bellville, Cheryl W. *Theater Magic Behind the Scenes at a Children's Theater.* Minneapolis, Minn.: Carolrhoda, 1986.

Block, James H., and King, Nancy R. *School Play: A Source Book.* New York, N.Y.: Garland, 1987.

Cornelison, Gayle, ed. *A Directory of Children's Theaters in the United States.* Lanham, Md.: University Press of America, 1983.

Davis, Jed H., and Evans, Mary J. *Theater, Children and Youth,* rev. ed. New Orleans, La.: Anchorage, 1987.

England, Alan. *Theater for the Young.* New York, N.Y.: St. Martin's Press, 1990.

Fisher, Aileen. *Year-Round Programs for Young Players.* Boston, Mass.: Plays, Inc., 1985.

Harmon, Renée. *How to Audition for Movies and TV.* New York, N.Y.: Walker, 1992.

Holte, Adrienne K., and Mayr, Grace A. *Putting on the School Play: A Complete Handbook.* Collegeville, Penn.: PH Enterprises, 1980.

Laughlin, Mildred K., et al. *Social Studies Readers Theater for Children.* Englewood, Col.: Libraries Unlimited, 1991.

McCaslin, Nellie. *Historical Guide to Children's Theater in America.* Westport, Conn.: Greenwood, 1987.

Malkin, Michael, and Malkin, Pamela. *Moving Towards Theater Stories: Theater Activities for Children.* Byron, Calif.: Front Row Experience, 1988.

Swortzell, Lowell, ed. *International Guide to Children's Theater and Education Theater: A Historical and Geographical Source Book.* Westport, Conn.: Greenwood, 1989.

Way, Brian. *Audience Participation Theater for Young People.* Boston, Mass.: Bakers Plays, 1990.

Walker Plays for Oral Reading—Classic Stories, American Plays, Holiday Plays, Mythology Plays. New York, N.Y.: Walker, 1992.

MAGAZINES

Young Actors: The Drama Magazine for Young People. Plays and dramatic programs for use in grades 1–12. Contact Plays, 120 Boylston Street, Boston, Mass. 02116-4615.

Exciting Plays for World History Class; Exciting Plays for Medieval History Class; and *Short Plays for American History Class.* J. Weston Walch, Publisher. 321 Valley Street, P.O. Box 658, Portland, Me. 04104-0658.

American Theatre Magazine. Curtis Brown and Associates, 10 Astor Place, New York, N.Y. 10013.

index

GAYLORD S